REGENTS ENGLISH WORKBOOK

Advanced

ROBERT J. DIXSON
ALLAN DART

D1713723

3

ADULT EDUCATION
YPSILANTI PUBLIC SCHOOLS
210 West Cross Street
Ypsilanti, Michigan 48197

REGENTS PUBLISHING COMPANY, INC.

Cover and text design: Finley/Wall Associates

ISBN 0-88345-674-5

Published by Regents Publishing Company, Inc.
2 Park Avenue
New York, New York 10016

Printed in the United States of America

10 9 8 7 6 5 4 3

To the Teacher

There is no need here to describe the different types of exercises which this book contains or to discuss their wide variety and extent. A glance through the following pages is enough to acquaint anyone with the book's general contents.

Since this is a workbook, there is also little to say as to how it should be used. Each exercise carries its own instructions, and the students proceed accordingly. On the other hand, there are a few points of general pedagogy which the teacher using the book should keep in mind.

First, this is a workbook, and all explanatory material has been kept to a minimum. Thus, the book is not designed to be used alone or to replace completely the regular classroom text. Rather, this book should be used to supplement the regular classroom text, to give needed variety to the lesson, or to provide additional drill materials on important points of grammar and usage.

Second, as a teacher using this book, don't assume that after students have written the answers to an exercise correctly, they know the material thoroughly and can use the principle in their everyday speech. The exercise is often only the beginning. Much drill and practice are still necessary. Therefore, ask questions or introduce simple conversation involving the particular grammar principle. Also, don't hesitate to repeat the exercises in the book several times. Run over these exercises orally in class. If the students have already written the answers in their books, they can cover these answers with their hand or with a separate sheet of paper. Continue to review past exercises which seem important to you or which have given the students difficulty.

Third, don't fall into the further error of assuming that some of the exercises in this book are too easy for your particular students. Certain exercises may seem easy to you—especially if you speak English as a native—but they still represent a real challenge to anyone studying English as a foreign language. In this connection, there is one additional point of utmost importance which should be kept in mind. We are not interested in these exercises in tricking or even in *testing* the student. The exercises are not designed to find out how much a student knows or does not know. Their purpose is simply to drill the student on certain basic points of grammar and usage. The exercises are practice exercises—nothing more. They provide just another means of having students repeat materials which can be learned only through continuous use. For this reason, a good deal of direct repetition has been purposely introduced, not only in individual exercises but throughout the book.

There are three workbooks in the series. Book 1 is for the beginning student; Book 2 is for the intermediate student; Book 3 is for the advanced student. As regards the exact division of material, this plan was followed:

The exercises in Book 1 more or less parallel the development by lesson of the material in *Beginning Lessons in English* A and B. Similarly, Book 2 follows the general development of the lessons in *Second Book in English*. Book 3 reviews the material in Books 1 and 2 and focuses on special problems on the advanced level. All the books mentioned are published by Regents Publishing Company.

Regents English Workbooks are readily adaptable to many uses and can serve effectively to supplement any standard classroom textbook. A perforated answer key at the back of the book makes classroom use or self-study equally feasible.

R.J.D.

Contents

Exercise Number
Page Number   Structure

1 To be: present tense

Full Form	Contraction	Full Form	Contraction
I am	I'm	we are	we're
you are	you're	you are	you're
he is	he's	they are	they're
she is	she's		
it is	it's		

A. **Supply the correct form of the present tense of** *to be* **as in the example. Use the contracted form.**

1. ___She's___ a good student. (she)

2. _____ good friends. (they)

3. _____ a beautiful day. (it)

4. _____ absent today. (he)

5. _____ good news. (it)

6. _____ brothers. (we)

7. _____ a doctor. (she)

8. _____ a foreign student. (I)

9. _____ a foreign student. (you)

10. _____ foreign students. (they)

B. **Supply the correct form of the present tense of** *to be* **as in the example. Use the full form.**

1. He ___is___ a good student.

2. Sheila _____ a business executive.

3. Today _____ Monday.

4. She and Taro _____ both good students.

5. The police officer _____ busy with the traffic.

6. He and I _____ old friends.

7. The light _____ out.

8. These books _____ yours.

9. Yellow _____ my favorite color.

10. Christmas _____ a joyous time of year.

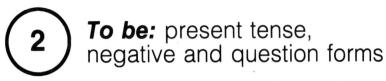

2 *To be:* present tense, negative and question forms

Form the negative by placing *not* after the verb. The contractions are *aren't* and *isn't.*

Form questions by placing the verb before the subject.

   Is she a lawyer?   No, she *isn't* a lawyer.

Change the statements to questions, and then give a negative answer as in the example.

1. They're in Europe now.
    a.   Are they in Europe now?
    b.   They aren't in Europe now.

2. Ricardo is angry with us.
    a. _____
    b. _____

3. He and she are good friends.
    a. _____
    b. _____

4. He is very happy.
    a. _____
    b. _____

5. Both sisters are tall and athletic.
    a. _____
    b. _____

6. She is a clever girl.
    a. _____
    b. _____

7. They are members of our club.
    a. _____
    b. _____

8. He is a good baseball player.
    a. _____
    b. _____

3 *To be:* past tense

I was	we were
you were	you were
he was	they were
she was	
it was	

Fill in the blank with the correct past tense form of *to be.*

1. Carlos _____was_____ absent from school last week.

2. I _____ in the same class as Sally last year.

3. We _____ good friends for many years.

4. The windows of the car _____ open.

5. Both doors _____ closed.

6. Mike _____ not at work yesterday.

7. They _____ sick.

8. You _____ not home last night when I called.

9. We _____ tired after our long walk.

10. I _____ hungry after so much work.

11. There _____ many students absent yesterday.

12. She _____ present at the lesson, but I _____ not.

13. The weather yesterday _____ very warm.

14. He _____ at his aunt's house all day.

15. The teacher _____ satisfied with my composition.

16. The exercises in the last lesson _____ easy.

17. We _____ sorry to see her leave.

18. The wind last night _____ very strong.

19. It _____ cold last night.

20. We _____ happy to hear the good news.

21. When I saw her, she _____ very happy.

22. Her face _____ full of happiness.

23. We _____ thrilled to hear about her success.

24. They _____ happy.

25. We ate the apples and thought they _____ delicious.

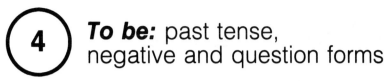

4 To be: past tense, negative and question forms

Form the negative by placing *not* after the verb. The contractions are *wasn't* and *weren't*. Form questions by placing the verb before the subject.

Was she a doctor?   She *wasn't* a doctor.

Change the following statements to questions, and then give a negative answer as in the example.

1. He was absent yesterday.
   a. Was he absent yesterday?
   b. He wasn't absent yesterday.

2. The doors were closed.
   a.
   b.

3. The exercises were difficult.
   a.
   b.

4. The woman was a stranger to her.
   a.
   b.

5. It was a beautiful day.
   a.
   b.

6. The sea was very calm.
   a.
   b.

7. He was a tall man.
   a.
   b.

8. There were many difficult exercises in the lesson.
   a.
   b.

5 *To be:* future tense

Full Form	Contraction	Full Form	Contraction
I will be	I'll be	we will be	we'll be
you will be	you'll be	you will be	you'll be
he will be	he'll be	they will be	they'll be
she will be	she'll be		
it will be	it'll be		

Change the following statements to the future tense. Use the contraction with personal pronouns.

1. He is at school.

   He'll be at school.

2. She is our new teacher.

3. Ms. Roth is in New York.

4. They are good students.

5. This is your desk.

6. There are two soldiers in the room.

7. We are very tired after a long walk.

8. I am happy to be here.

9. You are angry with us.

10. The dog is happy to see you.

11. Mr. Moreno is out of town.

12. The wine is very good this year.

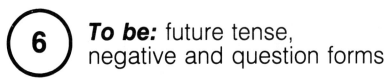

6 **To be:** future tense, negative and question forms

Form negatives by placing *not* after *will*. The contraction is *won't*. Form questions by placing *will* before the subject.

Will they be on time?   No, they *won't* be on time.

Change the following statements to the question form, and then give a negative answer as in the example.

1. She will be present tomorrow.

    a. ___Will she be present tomorrow?___

    b. ___She won't be present tomorrow.___

2. The test will be easy.

    a. _____

    b. _____

3. They will be here before noon.

    a. _____

    b. _____

4. There will be three tables in the room.

    a. _____

    b. _____

5. He will be happy to get home.

    a. _____

    b. _____

6. She will be very angry.

    a. _____

    b. _____

7. Mr. Murphy will be in class today.

    a. _____

    b. _____

8. Nicholas will be absent next week.

    a. _____

    b. _____

Present continuous tense

The present continuous tense describes an action which is going on at the moment of speaking and is not yet complete. Form the present continuous tense with the present tense of the verb *to be* and the present participle of the main verb.

I am working.   We are working.
(I'm working.)   (We're working.)
You are working.   You are working.
(You're working.)   (You're working.)
He is working.   They are working.
(He's working.)   (They're working.)
She is working.
(She's working.)
It is working.
(It's working.)

Fill in the blanks with the present continuous form of the verbs in parentheses. Use the contraction with personal pronouns.

1. <u>They're waiting</u> for us downstairs. (they, wait)

2. The bus _____ for us now. (stop)

3. I think the telephone _____ . (ring)

4. I see that _____ your new suit today. (you, wear)

5. Look! A deer _____ the road. (cross)

6. Listen! Someone _____ a car. (start)

7. Please be quiet! The baby _____ . (sleep)

8. Look! The cat _____ to climb that tall tree. (try)

9. Helen _____ good progress in her studies. (make)

10. The leaves _____ to fall from the trees. (begin)

11. Bertha _____ lunch in the cafeteria now. (have)

12. Listen! Pat _____ the piano. (play)

13. At present, _____ in South America. (they, live)

14. For the time being, Jack _____ this department. (manage)

15. Be careful! The teacher _____ you. (watch)

16. _____ sales in all the big stores now. (they, have)

17. Mother _____ the garden now. (water)

18. The Salazar family _____ the summer in Venezuela. (spend)

8 **Present continuous tense:**
negative and question forms

Form negatives in the present continuous tense by placing *not* **after** *to be.*
Form questions in the present continuous tense by placing *to be* **before the**
subject.

Is Daniel studying tonight?   No, he *isn't* studying tonight.

Change the following statements to the question form, and then give a
negative answer as in the example.

1. The telephone is ringing.
   a. <u>Is the telephone ringing?</u>
   b. <u>The telephone isn't ringing.</u>

2. It is beginning to rain.
   a. _____
   b. _____

3. The sky is growing dark.
   a. _____
   b. _____

4. He is working for a new company.
   a. _____
   b. _____

5. Pete is cleaning the room now.
   a. _____
   b. _____

6. The joggers are turning the corner.
   a. _____
   b. _____

7. She is having lunch outside on the lawn.
   a. _____
   b. _____

8. Nora is doing well in college.
   a. _____
   b. _____

Past continuous tense

The past continuous tense describes an action in the past that was going on when another action took place. Form the past continuous tense with the past tense of *to be* and the present participle of the main verb.

I was working.   We were working.
You were working.   You were working.
He was working.   They were working.
She was working.
It was working.

Fill in the blanks with the past continuous form of the verbs in parentheses.

1. They <u>were eating</u> in the restaurant when we called. (eat)

2. It _____ when I left home. (rain)

3. When you telephoned, I _____ dinner. (have)

4. They _____ in Europe when the war broke out. (travel)

5. The baby _____ soundly when I went to wake him. (sleep)

6. He _____ breakfast when I went to his hotel room. (order)

7. I got sick while we _____ to Mexico. (drive)

8. He _____ in California when his father died. (work)

9. I _____ a nap when you called. (take)

10. She _____ with Mr. Wong when I saw her in the hall. (talk)

11. The accident happened while they _____ in a hotel. (stay)

12. She fell as she _____ into a taxi. (get)

13. The car _____ slowly when it struck the child. (go)

14. When I got up this morning, the sun _____ brightly. (shine)

15. Annette _____ television when the storm began. (watch)

(10) Future continuous tense

The future continuous tense describes an action which will be going on in the future. Form the future continuous tense with the future tense of the verb *to be* and the present participle of the main verb.

I will be working.
(I'll be working.)
You will be working.
(You'll be working.)
He will be working.
(He'll be working.)
She will be working.
(She'll be working.)
It will be working.
(It'll be working.)

We will be working.
(We'll be working.)
You will be working.
(You'll be working.)
They will be working.
(They'll be working.)

Fill in the blanks with the future continuous form of the verbs in parentheses. Use the contraction with personal pronouns.

1. If you come at noon, _we'll be eating_ lunch. (we, eat)

2. At this time next month, _____ in South America. (you, travel)

3. At ten o'clock tomorrow morning, _____ my music lesson. (I, have)

4. _____ for you on the corner at the usual time tomorrow morning. (I, wait)

5. If you call her at six, _____ the piano. (she, practice)

6. _____ when you get back. (it, rain)

7. If you arrive before six, _____ in my garden. (I, work)

8. Tomorrow afternoon at this time, _____ over the Caribbean Sea. (we, fly)

9. Don't call him between seven and eight. _____ his favorite television program. (he, watch)

10. Don't call her before four. _____ her usual afternoon nap. (she, take)

11. At this time next year, _____ at Columbia University. (he, study)

12. If we go there now, _____ dinner. (they, have)

13. But if we go later, _____ television. (they, watch)

14. At this time tomorrow afternoon, _____ my final English examination. (I, take)

Simple present tense

The simple present tense describes an action which goes on every day or in general.

I work	we work
you work	you work
he works	they work
she works	
it works	

Fill in the blanks with the present tense form of the verb in parentheses.

1. We ___read___ the newspaper every day. (read)

2. He _____ to school by bus. (come)

3. I always _____ to school. (walk)

4. The children _____ in the park every afternoon. (play)

5. I _____ lunch in the cafeteria every day. (eat)

6. Sue _____ very hard. (work)

7. I _____ to sit in the sun. (like)

8. The dog _____ the cat all around the house. (chase)

9. Ms. Glenfield _____ at the clinic. (work)

10. Joan generally _____ at this desk. (sit)

11. We always _____ tennis on Saturdays. (play)

12. He always _____ his homework carefully. (prepare)

13. They _____ lunch together every day. (eat)

14. My son _____ to play video games. (like)

15. They _____ many trips together. (take)

16. We always _____ by car. (travel)

17. Her family _____ church every Sunday. (attend)

18. She _____ several foreign languages. (speak)

19. They _____ to the park as often as they can. (go)

20. He _____ the garden every day. (water)

21. My boss _____ every Wednesday. (jog)

22. She _____ her mind often. (change)

23. Jack always _____ his time. (take)

(12) Simple present tense: negative form

Form the negative of the simple present tense by placing *do not* or *does not* before the simple form of the verb. The contractions are *don't* and *doesn't.*

> I do not know.   He does not know.
>   (I don't know.)   (He doesn't know.)

A. Change the following statements to the negative form. Use the full form.

1. I work on the tenth floor.

   <u>I do not work on the tenth floor.</u>

2. Ann likes to study English.

   _____

3. They speak French well.

   _____

4. The plane leaves at ten o'clock.

   _____

5. He knows French perfectly.

   _____

6. I feel well today.

   _____

B. Change the following statements to the negative form. Use the contracted form.

1. They live in Chicago.

   <u>They don't live in Chicago.</u>

2. I need air conditioning in my room.

   _____

3. We use many books every year.

   _____

4. I understand everything he says.

   _____

5. She wants to visit Mexico.

   _____

6. He begins his new job on the fifteenth.

   _____

Form questions in the simple present tense by placing *do* **or** *does* **before the subject.**

Do I go?   Do we go?
Do you go?   Do you go?
Does he go?   Do they go?
Does she go?
Does it go?

Change the following statements to the question form.

1. They speak English well.
   <u>Do they speak English well?</u>

2. He enjoys fishing.

3. She spends her vacation in the mountains.

4. They come to school by bus.

5. Andrew knows how to play soccer.

6. The children wake up at about six o'clock every morning.

7. He knows a lot about South America.

8. They go to the park every afternoon.

9. They have many friends in that school.

10. Both boys swim well.

11. They live on the outskirts of the city.

12. Roy gets up early every morning.

14 **Regular verbs:** past tense

The past tense describes an action which occurred at a definite time in the past. Form the past tense of regular verbs by adding *ed* to the simple form of the verb.

I worked.	We worked.
You worked.	You worked.
He worked.	They worked.
She worked.	
It worked.	

Fill in the blanks with the past tense form of the verb in parentheses.

1. We ___worked___ in our garden yesterday. (work)

2. I _____ to the radio until twelve o'clock last night. (listen)

3. Yoshiko and I _____ by telephone yesterday. (talk)

4. He always _____ to learn English. (want)

5. They _____ in France for many years. (live)

6. We _____ to go to Europe in June. (expect)

7. The meeting _____ about two hours. (last)

8. Mrs. Walker _____ trains in New York. (change)

9. We both _____ the movie last night very much. (like)

10. I _____ almost two hours for Tom and Lynn. (wait)

11. They _____ their house white. (paint)

12. Daniel _____ late for class. (arrive)

13. We _____ television until eleven o'clock last night. (watch)

14. She _____ in our class last semester. (study)

15. I _____ your letter on my way to work. (mail)

16. We both _____ how to swim many years ago. (learn)

17. The boy _____ the groceries early in the morning. (deliver)

18. She _____ her confidence in her best friend. (place)

19. Carol _____ all the way to the store. (walk)

20. Mother _____ a wonderful dinner last night. (cook)

21. I _____ to her as she got on the plane. (wave)

22. Josh _____ his final examination. (pass)

23. He _____ the radio and went to sleep. (turn off)

24. They _____ to another town. (move)

Irregular verbs: past tense

The irregular past tense uses the same form for all persons.

I wrote	we wrote
you wrote	you wrote
he wrote	they wrote
she wrote	
it wrote	

Fill in the blanks with the past tense form of the verb in parentheses.

1. Ms. Burns ___came___ to visit us last night. (come)
2. They _____ us about their plans for the new home. (tell)
3. The weather was warm, so we _____ on our front porch. (sit)
4. I _____ your hat and coat in the next room. (put)
5. The meeting last night _____ at eight and ended at ten. (begin)
6. I stayed home last night and _____ several letters. (write)
7. He _____ Angela on the street yesterday. (see)
8. This book _____ two dollars. (cost)
9. I __had__ my lunch in the cafeteria at noon. (have)
10. The man __brak__ a lot of wine at the party last night. (drink)
11. I _____ John your message. (give)
12. Mrs. Reese finally __sold__ her house. (sell)
13. Anne _____ the president speak on television last night. (hear)
14. My father _____ Mr. Evans well. (know)
15. Dolores _____ very well yesterday, but today she feels sick again. (feel) _d_
16. We __went__ to the park yesterday. (go)
17. I _____ that novel several years ago. (read)
18. She __spoke__ to me as soon as she __came__ in. (speak, come)
19. Dennis __wrote__ her and __told__ her the news. (write, tell)
20. The teacher __knew__ my name. (know)

Knew

(16) Past tense: negative form

Form the negative in the past tense by placing *did not* **before the simple form of the verb. The contraction is** *didn't.*

I did not work. (I didn't work.)

A. **Change the following statements to the negative using the full form** *did not.*

1. He wrote his lesson.

   He did not write his lesson.

2. They told us the story.

   _____

3. She put the books on his desk.

   _____

4. We stayed in Mexico City for two weeks.

   _____

5. I saw Florence yesterday.

   _____

6. He planned his work well.

   _____

B. **Change the following statements to the negative using the contraction** *didn't.*

1. The man fainted in the heat.

   The man didn't faint in the heat.

2. I knew him very well.

   _____

3. You sold your new car.

   _____

4. Mr. Wood spoke to Beth about the exam.

   _____

5. She came to the meeting alone.

   _____

6. We sat together at the concert last night.

   _____

17 **Past tense:** question form

Form questions in the past tense by placing *did* before the subject.

Did I work?	Did we work?
Did you work?	Did you work?
Did he work?	Did they work?
Did she work?	
Did it work?	

Change the following statements to the question form.

1. She worked all day.
   Did she work all day?

2. Don gave her a VCR for Christmas.

3. We stayed in Europe all year.

4. She told us about her trip.

5. He entered this class in September.

6. They went by plane.

7. She came home very late.

8. They went to the party together.

9. They knew each other as children.

10. Rose worked there for many years.

11. Mr. Stein felt better after his operation.

12. The meeting began on time.

(18) Future tense

The future tense expresses promise or determination. Form the future tense by placing *will* before the simple form of the verb.

Full Form	*Contraction*	*Full Form*	*Contraction*
I will go.	I'll go.	We will go.	We'll go.
You will go.	You'll go.	You will go.	You'll go.
He will go.	He'll go.	They will go.	They'll go.
She will go.	She'll go.		
It will go.	It'll go.		

Fill in the blanks with the future tense form of the verb in parentheses. Use the contracted form with personal pronouns.

1. __He'll call__ you tomorrow. (he, call)

2. _____ us in the morning. (they, see)

3. _____ you that money tomorrow. (I, give)

4. _____ you with that work. (she, help)

5. Mary _____ the table right away. (clean)

6. The stores _____ early today. (close)

7. _____ the tip. (I, leave)

8. Barbara _____ the book which you need. (find)

9. _____ a place to stay. (you, need)

10. Kevin _____ well in that job. (do)

11. The wind _____ that sign down. (blow)

12. _____ you in Grand Central Station. (we, meet)

13. _____ the bill. (I, pay)

14. _____ a great deal in that course. (you, learn)

15. _____ in Mexico about a month. (we, remain)

16. His secretary says that _____ back at six o'clock. (he, be)

17. Sonia _____ the cashier. (pay)

18. _____ a lot of money there. (you, spend)

19. _____ you a cup of tea. (I, make)

20. I'm sure _____ the book you lost. (you, find)

21. My boss _____ me a raise next week. (give)

22. The stores _____ at nine o'clock. (open)

23. _____ in New York for about a week. (we, be)

18

(19) **Future tense:** negative form

Form negatives in the future tense by placing *not* after *will* or by using the contraction *won't* before the main verb.

I will not go.   (I won't go.)

A. **Change the following statements to the negative form using the full form *will not*.**

1. They will arrive at three o'clock.
   <u>They will not arrive at three o'clock.</u>

2. My boyfriend will finish his degree next year.
   _____

3. I will be back tomorrow.
   _____

4. The weather will be cool tomorrow.
   _____

5. Tom will be able to meet us this evening.
   _____

6. These exercises will be difficult for you.
   _____

B. **Change the following statements to the negative form using the contraction *won't*.**

1. You will be there before dawn.
   <u>You won't be there before dawn.</u>

2. She will do well in that position.
   _____

3. Gina will teach all the grammar courses.
   _____

4. Jim and I will sign the contract tomorrow.
   _____

5. They will finish the work in April.
   _____

6. The meeting will last an hour.
   _____

20 Future tense: question form

Form questions in the future tense by placing *will* before the subject.

Will I go?	Will we go?
Will you go?	Will you go?
Will he go?	Will they go?
Will she go?	
Will it go?	

Change the following statements to the question form.

1. They will arrive on Wednesday.
   Will they arrive on Wednesday?

2. Ned will come back at three o'clock.

3. The shop will be open at six o'clock.

4. It will cost six dollars to fix the lamp.

5. The plant will die without sunshine.

6. They will spend four months in Spain.

7. She will meet us downtown.

8. They will pay their bill next week.

9. The meeting will begin at eight.

10. It will last an hour.

21 Going to future

The *going to* future describes some definite future action. Form the *going to* future with the appropriate form of *to be going to* and the simple form of the verb.

I am going to work.	We are going to work.
You are going to work.	You are going to work.
He is going to work.	They are going to work.
She is going to work.	
It is going to work.	

Fill in the blanks with the *going to* future form of the verb in parentheses.

1. They _are going to visit_ us tomorrow. (visit)

2. We _____ dinner in town tonight. (have)

3. I _____ to Disneyland this summer. (go)

4. He _____ for New York in the morning. (leave)

5. She _____ her family in Virginia. (visit)

6. You _____ at the meeting tonight. (speak)

7. Danny _____ Russian next year. (study)

8. Andrew _____ an examination on Wednesday. (take)

9. They _____ for us after the movie. (wait)

10. We _____ to Chicago. (fly)

11. Pedro _____ to be a doctor. (study)

12. We _____ up early tomorrow and go fishing. (get)

13. You and I _____ to Canada on our vacation. (go)

14. She _____ for Europe soon. (leave)

15. They _____ that whole block of buildings. (tear down)

16. Joan _____ to town to buy some new dresses. (go)

17. They _____ their present home and buy a new one. (sell)

18. Mrs. Jacobs _____ the children to the zoo this afternoon. (take)

19. They _____ some new clothes for their vacation. (buy)

20. The children _____ their chores after breakfast. (do)

21. Their father _____ them. (help)

22. While they're doing their chores, I _____ the dishes. (wash)

22 *Going to* future:
negative and question forms

Form negatives in the *going to* **future by placing** *not* **after** *to be.*

I am going to work.   I'm *not* going to work.

Form questions in the *going to* **future by placing** *to be* **before the subject.**

You are going to work.   *Are* you going to work?

Change these statements to questions, and then give a negative answer as in the example. Use the contracted form of pronoun + *to be* **.**

1. They are going to wait for us.
   a. _Are they going to wait for us?_
   b. _They're not going to wait for us._

2. Rose is going to take a vacation.
   a. _____
   b. _____

3. We are going to go to the movies tonight.
   a. _____
   b. _____

4. He is going to start working there on Monday.
   a. _____
   b. _____

5. They are going to pay him a good salary.
   a. _____
   b. _____

6. Carmen is going to move to California next month.
   a. _____
   b. _____

7. Henry is going to travel to Europe on his vacation.
   a. _____
   b. _____

8. She is going to spend the weekend in Connecticut.
   a. _____
   b. _____

(23) Present perfect tense

The present perfect tense describes a past action connected with the present time. Form the present perfect tense by placing *have/has* before the past participle of the verb.

I have worked.
  (I've worked.)
You have worked.
  (You've worked.)
He has worked.
  (He's worked.)
She has worked.
  (She's worked.)
It has worked.
  (It's worked.)

We have worked.
  (We've worked.)
You have worked.
  (You've worked.)
They have worked.
  (They've worked.)

Fill in the blanks with the present perfect form of the verb in parentheses.

1. I _have spoken_ to him about it several times. (speak)
2. We _____ all our homework. (finish)
3. He _____ us many times. (visit)
4. She _____ my book at last. (return)
5. I am afraid that I _____ my car keys. (lose)
6. We _____ in Mexico many times. (be)
7. I _____ this exercise before. (study)
8. We _____ many new words in this course. (learn)
9. My family _____ to Montreal. (be)
10. I _____ that story before. (hear)
11. We _____ money to them several times. (lend)
12. Mr. Petridis _____ to South America to work. (go)
13. His uncle _____ computer science for years. (teach)
14. She _____ that movie three times. (see)
15. He _____ and _____ several fortunes. (make, lose)
16. Kelly _____ that recipe many times. (try)
17. He _____ to understand what Alice wants. (begin)
18. The flowers _____ very high. (grew)
19. They _____ in Acapulco many times. (be)
20. Dick _____ them in Mexico twice. (visit)

(24) Present perfect tense:
negative and question forms

Form questions with the present perfect tense by placing *have/has* before the subject.

Form the negative of the present perfect tense by placing *not* after *have/has*. The contractions are *haven't* and *hasn't*.

He has seen it.   Has he seen it?   He hasn't seen it.

Change these statements to questions, and then give a negative answer as in the example. Use the contraction of *have/has* + *not*.

1. He has worked very hard.
   a. ___Has he worked very hard?___
   b. ___He hasn't worked very hard.___

2. She has been there for many years.
   a. _____
   b. _____

3. They have waited there a long time.
   a. _____
   b. _____

4. The movie has been seen by millions of people.
   a. _____
   b. _____

5. Mr. and Mrs. Sato have studied English.
   a. _____
   b. _____

6. Alan has been absent.
   a. _____
   b. _____

7. They have found a pen.
   a. _____
   b. _____

8. He has been the best student all year.
   a. _____
   b. _____

25 Present perfect continuous tense

Form the present perfect continuous tense by placing *have/has* **or its contracted form before** *been* **plus the present participle of the verb.**

I have been working.	We have been working.
(I've been working.)	You have been working.
You have been working.	They have been working.
He has been working.	
(He's been working.)	
She has been working.	
It has been working.	

In some cases, the present perfect continuous tense can be used interchangeably with the present perfect tense.

Change the following statements to the present perfect continuous tense.

1. She has worked there for many years.
   She has been working there for many years.

2. He has sold cars for many years.
   _____

3. They have traveled all over Europe.
   _____

4. She has slept for more than ten hours.
   _____

5. It has rained all day long.
   _____

6. He has studied English for many years.
   _____

7. She has caught fish in that stream for years.
   _____

8. He has taught English for ten years.
   _____

9. They have lived in Caracas since 1983.
   _____

10. The two nations have quarreled for many years.
    _____

(26) Past perfect tense

The past perfect tense describes an action which took place before a definite time in the past. It is often used with the past tense. Form the past perfect tense by placing *had ('d)* before the past participle of the verb.

I had seen (I'd seen)	we had seen
you had seen	you had seen
he had seen	they had seen
she had seen	
it had seen	

Fill in the blanks with the past perfect form of the verb in parentheses.

1. The professor ___had left___ by the time we arrived. (leave)

2. He told me that he _____ everywhere for us. (look)

3. Before coming to us, he _____ in sales. (work)

4. It was Roberta who told me that the police _____ the thief. (capture)

5. The teacher returned the exercises we _____ for her. (prepare)

6. She said that she _____ them to be fairly good. (find)

7. I met them before I _____ a hundred yards. (go)

8. He _____ there for just a week when the accident happened. (work)

9. I saw that we _____ the wrong road. (take)

10. They told me that Henry _____ the class. (leave)

11. She insisted that she _____ that movie. (see)

12. Somehow I felt that I _____ the man before. (meet)

13. She said that she _____ her lunch. (have)

14. Previously, he _____ a very good student. (be)

15. It was clear that someone _____ us. (misdirect)

16. He asked me why I _____ the party so early. (leave)

17. I asked him what countries he _____ . (visit)

18. The child wanted to know what _____ to her ice cream. (happen)

19. The apartment was smaller than we _____ . (expect)

20. I was surprised to hear that they _____ to move away. (decide)

26

(27) Past perfect continuous tense

The past perfect continuous tense describes a continuing action that ended at the time of the past tense verb of the sentence or before. Form the past perfect continuous tense by placing *had* before *been* plus the present participle of the verb. *Had* can be contracted with all the personal pronouns except *it*.

I had been working.
(I'd been working.)
You had been working.
(You'd been working.)
He had been working.
(He'd been working.)
She had been working.
(She'd been working.)
It had been working.

We had been working.
(We'd been working.)
You had been working.
(You'd been working.)
They had been working.
(They'd been working.)

Fill in the blanks with the past perfect continuous form of the verb in parentheses.

1. Because of the smoke, I could tell that someone <u>had been smoking</u> a cigarette. (smoke)

2. When we arrived, she was studying, but she _____ television. (watch)

3. I _____ in Kyoto for ten years when I moved to Tokyo. (live)

4. When the police stopped the car, they asked the driver if he _____ . (drink)

5. I knew that she _____ because her hair was still wet. (swim)

6. He said that he had a tan because he _____ in the sun. (lie)

7. He finally collapsed because he _____ twelve-hour days for weeks. (work)

8. Nobody thought the elevator was dangerous because they _____ up and down in it safely for years. (go)

9. The car _____ well for months before the accident. (run)

10. Alice won the tennis match, although she _____ more golf than tennis. (play)

11. By the time I finished my shopping, I _____ for three hours. (walk)

(28) Future perfect tense

Form the future perfect tense by placing *will ('ll) have* before the past participle of the verb.

I will have gone.   We will have gone.
  (I'll have gone.)   You will have gone.
You will have gone.   They will have gone.
He will have gone.
She will have gone.
It will have gone.

Fill in the blanks with the future perfect form of the verb in parentheses.

1. When you arrive, they __will have left__ . (leave)

2. By August, the flowers _____ . (die)

3. If you come at noon tomorrow, I _____ the work. (finish)

4. If she gets here at six o'clock, they _____ . (go)

5. If he doesn't hurry, they _____ when he comes. (leave)

6. We _____ this book by June. (finish)

7. I _____ in this country two years next June. (be)

8. By tomorrow, I _____ all these rules. (forget)

9. By the time she finishes college, she _____ many things. (learn)

10. You _____ all about it by this time next year. (forget)

11. Before he leaves, he _____ every show in town. (see)

12. She _____ by two o'clock. (arrive)

13. By the time we get there, they _____ the lesson. (finish)

14. All the trees _____ their leaves by winter. (lost)

15. By the time Carlos leaves New York, he _____ many interesting things. (do)

16. I am sure they _____ the new road by January. (complete)

17. She says that before she leaves, she _____ at every restaurant in town. (eat)

18. All the leaves _____ color by fall. (change)

19. A century from now, wars _____ a thing of the past. (become)

Review: verb tenses

This is a review of all of the tenses that have been studied so far in this text. Fill in the blank with the correct tense of the verb in parentheses.

1. Andy ___comes___ to class on time. (come)
2. Kathy _____ us at present. (teach)
3. I _____ in my garden when you called me yesterday. (work)
4. We _____ our examinations next week. (have)
5. I _____ to work on the bus this morning. (come)
6. As I _____ to work this morning, I _____ a beggar who _____ me for some money. (come, meet, ask)
7. I _____ to Radio City several times. (be)
8. Listen! I think someone _____ the piano. (play)
9. Paula said that she _____ that movie previously. (see)
10. I _____ that novel three or four times. (read)
11. By this time next year, we _____ all the courses. (complete)
12. Your telegram _____ just as I _____ my house. (come, leave)
13. The sun _____ brightly when I got up this morning. (shine)
14. Our class _____ every morning at eight-thirty. (begin)
15. We occasionally _____ to the movies on Sunday. (go)
16. Hey, someone _____ on the door. (knock)
17. Up to now, nothing _____ from the lost pilots. (hear)
18. Jorge _____ English for two years. (study)
19. Alma _____ French for a few months last year. (study)
20. My brother _____ to visit me next week. (come)
21. When you telephoned me, I _____ my lesson. (study)
22. While we _____ to Chicago, we _____ two flat tires. (drive, have)
23. Sue _____ from her seat the minute the bell rang. (jump)
24. When we got home, we discovered that Rose _____ and _____ a message on our machine. (call, leave)
25. Mr. Fitzpatrick _____ as he _____ the street. (fall, cross)

(30) Review: negative form

Change these affirmative statements to negative ones. Use contractions wherever possible.

1. She speaks English well.
   <u>She doesn't speak English well.</u>

2. We went to the movies last night.
   _____

3. You ought to tell him.
   _____

4. He should go there sooner.
   _____

5. I have lived there for many years.
   _____

6. They were supposed to leave yesterday.
   _____

7. She can speak French perfectly.
   _____

8. The mechanic will be back by eight o'clock.
   _____

9. He had to work late last night.
   _____

10. My friend lives in Los Angeles.
    _____

11. She is the best student in our class.
    _____

12. You may smoke here.
    _____

13. There were many students absent from class yesterday.
    _____

14. They were driving very fast at the time.
    _____

Review: question form 1

Change these statements to questions.

1. They must go home.
   <u>Must they go home?</u>

2. Mr. Ralston can speak Chinese fluently.
   _____

3. She should spend more time at home.
   _____

4. He may sit in this chair.
   _____

5. They can meet us in Los Angeles.
   _____

6. Her brother-in-law can't drive.
   _____

7. Ruth should eat less candy.
   _____

8. You must tell her the truth.
   _____

9. We should speak to her about it.
   _____

10. They may leave now.
    _____

11. The entire tour group can go by van.
    _____

12. You must send them a telegram.
    _____

13. She should work at home.
    _____

14. She may wait in the office.
    _____

Change the following statements to questions using the question words in parentheses.

1. They live in New York. (where)
   <u>Where do they live?</u>

2. There are twelve months in a year. (how many)
   _____

3. She may wait in the hall. (where)
   _____

4. The jet arrived at noon. (what time)
   _____

5. It is six o'clock now. (what time)
   _____

6. He went to Chicago by plane. (how)
   _____

7. She must leave at five. (what time)
   _____

8. They are in the Oval Office right now. (where)
   _____

9. The book cost five dollars. (how much)
   _____

10. They work in Mexico now. (where)
    _____

11. Her supervisor lived in Tokyo for two years. (how long)
    _____

12. He got up at five o'clock this morning. (what time)
    _____

13. They sat in the park for two hours. (how long)
    _____

14. She understands English very well. (how well)
    _____

(33) Contractions

Contractions are used a great deal in everyday spoken English. Study them, and try to use them in a natural way.

Fill in the blanks with the contracted form of the words in parentheses.

1. ___He's___ a good student. (he is)
2. _____ waiting for us. (they are)
3. _____ be back before noon. (I will)
4. _____ lost my keys. (I have)
5. _____ rent a car in Santo Domingo. (we will)
6. _____ surely finish the work today. (she will)
7. _____ old friends. (we are)
8. _____ planning to leave next week. (they are)
9. _____ almost three o'clock. (it is)
10. Answer the phone. _____ ringing. (it is)
11. _____ just left. (they have)
12. We'll miss the train! _____ leaving the station. (it is)
13. _____ someone at the door. (there is)
14. _____ going to remain in Europe all summer. (she is)
15. _____ a big boy for his age. (he is)
16. _____ very kind to say that. (you are)
17. _____ glad that you were able to come. (I am)
18. _____ nothing we can do about it now. (there is)
19. _____ come back when they can. (they will)
20. _____ beginning to snow hard. (it is)
21. _____ need a winter coat in Vermont. (you will)

(34) Short answers

Write affirmative and negative short answers for the questions below. Answer *you* questions with *I* and *I* questions with *you*.

1. Can you speak French?

   a. _Yes, I can._   b. _No, I can't._

2. Does she live in San Francisco?

   a. _____   b. _____

3. Have you been sick?

   a. _____   b. _____

4. Is the lesson over?

   a. _____   b. _____

5. Will the Kollers be there, too?

   a. _____   b. _____

6. Are they going out?

   a. _____   b. _____

7. Did she study?

   a. _____   b. _____

8. Was the room warm?

   a. _____   b. _____

9. Is it raining now?

   a. _____   b. _____

10. Should we go home?

    a. _____   b. _____

11. May I smoke?

    a. _____   b. _____

12. Can your cousin Tim drive a truck?

    a. _____   b. _____

13. Did it rain yesterday?

    a. _____   b. _____

(35) Tag questions

A tag question is added to the end of a statement. If the sentence is affirmative, the tag question is negative.

He can speak English, *can't he?*
This bus goes downtown, *doesn't it?*

If the sentence is negative, the tag question is affirmative.

He can't speak English, *can he?*
This bus doesn't go downtown, *does it?*

Tag questions are usually added to confirm information already known by the speaker.

Fill in the blanks with tag questions.

1. He was in Italy, __wasn't he__?
2. Claire speaks fluent Spanish, _____?
3. That chair wasn't broken yesterday, _____?
4. It hasn't stopped raining for a week, _____?
5. My car is getting old, _____?
6. You are not very good at languages, _____?
7. There'll be enough ice cream for everyone, _____?
8. Sophie seemed pleased with the results of our examinations, _____?
9. It has been a very hot day, _____?
10. You won't see him again until next month, _____?
11. He always gets up early, _____?
12. You didn't get to bed very early last night, _____?
13. She can't dance as well as her sister, _____?
14. They dance well together, _____?
15. You are going with us to the movie, _____?
16. You know Ana's brother Sandro, _____?
17. Beds aren't very expensive, _____?
18. The dress is really not becoming to her, _____?
19. He couldn't understand a single word I said, _____?
20. I paid you, _____?
21. The plant hasn't died, _____?

36 Infinitives:
continuous and perfect forms

Form the continuous infinitive by placing *to be* before the present participle of the verb. The continuous infinitive describes an action occurring at the time of the main verb of the sentences.

He seems *to be making* good progress.
She seems too old *to be doing* that work.

Form the perfect infinitive by placing *to have* before the past participle of the verb. The perfect infinitive describes an action which occurred at a time earlier than that of the main verb of the sentence.

I am sorry *to have made* such a mistake.
I am glad *to have met* you.

A. **Fill in the blanks with the continuous form of the infinitive in parentheses.**

1. She seems <u>to be finding</u> the work easy. (find)

2. He appears _____ his classes. (enjoy)

3. I have _____ something every minute. (do)

4. You ought _____ more time on your English. (spend)

5. Vincent appears _____ his best. (do)

6. They are said _____ fast. (learn)

7. He is supposed _____ in the next room. (work)

8. She seems _____ trouble with that problem. (have)

9. I prefer _____ something more useful. (do)

B. **Fill in the blanks with the perfect form of the infinitive in parentheses.**

1. They are supposed <u>to have come</u> home early. (come)

2. I am pleased _____ you. (meet)

3. She would like _____ a video. (make)

4. He is supposed _____ already. (arrive)

5. My boyfriend seems _____ himself very much. (enjoy)

6. I am sorry not _____ this matter better. (understand)

7. They are certainly glad _____ that train. (miss)

8. Scott is sorry _____ practice today. (miss)

9. The output of the plant is said _____ a million tons a year. (be)

(37) Infinitives without *to*

When it is necessary to indicate a second action after the verbs *make*, *let*, *hear*, *see*, *watch*, and *feel*, use the infinitive without *to*.

He made us *wait* a long time.
She let us *go* home early.
No one saw him *leave*.

Use an infinitive without *to* after *but* and *except*.

We did nothing but *laugh*.
She never does anything except *complain*.

After the verb *help*, the infinitive with or without *to* may be used.

He helped me *to move* the chairs.
He helped me *move* the chairs.

Fill in the blanks with the correct form of the infinitive in parentheses.

1. The teacher let us __leave__ early. (leave)
2. The doctor made us _____ three hours. (wait)
3. I need _____ him the money. (take)
4. Will you help me _____ for the book? (look)
5. He wouldn't let me _____ in. (come)
6. We prefer _____ in the morning. (leave)
7. Did you hear him _____? (leave)
8. No one saw her _____ . (fall)
9. How long did he make you _____? (wait)
10. Don't let him _____ those things. (touch)
11. The nurse made us _____ the medicine. (take)
12. She seems _____ that we are going. (know)
13. Have you heard him _____ the piano? (play)
14. He helped me _____ the book. (write)
15. Everyone heard them _____ . (laugh)
16. David appears _____ upset. (be)
17. I watched him _____ the game. (play)
18. Let me _____ your composition. (see)

38 Passive voice 1

Form the passive voice with *to be* and the past participle of the main verb. There is a passive form for each of the active tenses in English.

Active Voice	*Passive Voice*
She brings the mail.	The mail is brought (by her).
She brought the mail.	The mail was brought.
She will bring the mail.	The mail will be brought.
She has brought the mail.	The mail has been brought.

Change the following statements from the active voice to the passive voice. Use a *by* phrase only in numbers 2, 10, and 13.

1. They educated him in Europe.

   He was educated in Europe.
   _____

2. He carried the heavy box.

   _____

3. The people recognized the president immediately.

   _____

4. Someone has stolen my umbrella.

   _____

5. They will deliver the merchandise in the morning.

   _____

6. Ms. Davis had already finished the portrait.

   _____

7. They finished the work in time.

   _____

8. We heard the cries of wolves in the distance.

   _____

9. The hunters found a young tiger in the open field.

   _____

10. The shot frightened the tiger.

    _____

11. They will bring some water from the well.

    _____

39 Passive voice 2

When a verb in the active voice has both a direct and an indirect object, the indirect object can become the subject when the sentence is changed to the passive form.

They gave *him* a present of a hundred dollars.
He was given a present of a hundred dollars.

They told *us* exactly where to sit.
We were told exactly where to sit.

Change these sentences to the passive voice. Make the indirect object the subject of the new sentence. Do not use a *by* phrase.

1. She told me the story.
   I was told the story.

2. They taught us two languages.

3. She asked us to come early.

4. The police gave the man a reward of a hundred dollars.

5. Our committee will send her flowers.

6. The guide showed us the principal spots of interest.

7. A friend told me the news.

8. We have asked everyone the same question.

9. Someone informed the police of his whereabouts.

10. Our boss has promised each of us a raise.

11. The officer will surely ask us about the accident.

(40) Passive voice: continuous form

Form the passive voice of the continuous tenses with the continuous form of *to be* and the past participle of the main verb.

Active Voice	*Passive Voice*
He is writing the letter.	The letter is being written.
She was fixing the car.	The car was being fixed.

Change the following statements from the active voice to the passive voice. Do not use a *by* phrase.

1. They are putting the car away.
   <u>The car is being put away.</u>

2. The organization was sending him to school.
   _____

3. We are arguing the case now.
   _____

4. They are building a new subway in that city.
   _____

5. He is putting some chairs in that room now, isn't he?
   _____

6. They are writing a letter now, aren't they?
   _____

7. They are tearing down the building across the street.
   _____

8. The gardener is watering the plants.
   _____

9. The jury is discussing the verdict now.
   _____

10. They were constructing many new buildings in Caracas when I was there.
    _____

11. The lawyers are drawing up both contracts today.
    _____

12. They are keeping the streets much cleaner now.
    _____

Passive voice:
modal auxiliaries

With modal auxiliaries like *can, may, must, have to, ought to,* and *should,* form the passive voice with *be* and the past participle of the main verb.

Active Voice	*Passive Voice*
He can carry the box.	The box can be carried.
She has to move her car.	Her car has to be moved.

Change these statements to the passive voice. Do not use a *by* phrase.

1. We must finish those letters.
   Those letters must be finished.

2. They should send the box to Philadelphia.
   _____

3. We have to start the engine first.
   _____

4. We may organize a new group.
   _____

5. I ought to cancel my appointment.
   _____

6. They cannot hold the meeting in that room.
   _____

7. The store may deliver the mattress while you're out.
   _____

8. Sheila has to pay the bill by the first of the month.
   _____

9. She must pay the other bills by the end of the month.
   _____

10. You ought to water the plants once a week.
    _____
    *the plants ought to be
    watered once a week.*

42 Passive voice: negative form

Form negatives with the passive voice by placing *not* after the auxiliary.

The class is *not* taught by Mr. Molina.
The thief was *not* caught by the police.

When two auxiliaries are used, *not* **always follows the first auxiliary.**

The stereo will *not* be delivered until tomorrow.
The ship had *not* been sunk by the enemy.

Change the following statements to the negative form.

1. The book was published.
   <u>The book was not published.</u>

2. My history teacher was born in Philadelphia.
   _____

3. The garden was watered.
   _____

4. The mail is delivered at ten o'clock.
   _____

5. His car was stolen from in front of his house.
   _____

6. The goods will be delivered on Wednesday.
   _____

7. The thief was sent to prison.
   _____

8. The president is elected every four years.
   _____

9. The children were put to bed.
   _____

10. The battle will be fought tomorrow.
    _____

11. The table has been moved.
    _____

12. She was given the best grade.
    _____

(43) **Passive voice:** question form

Form questions in the passive voice by placing the auxiliary verb before the subject.

Is the table made of marble?
Will the sofa be delivered by tomorrow?
Must the checks be signed right now?

Change the following statements to questions.

1. The town is located near a lake.
   <u>Is the town located near a lake?</u>

2. She is interested in Spanish.
   _____

3. They will be worn out after such a long trip.
   _____

4. Donna is interested in teaching aerobics.
   _____

5. They are concerned about his lack of strength.
   _____

6. Dave will be anxious to hear the rest of the story.
   _____

7. The stores are always closed at this hour.
   _____

8. The electricity has been turned off.
   _____

9. Both doors were closed.
   _____

10. He was very much discouraged by his failures.
    _____

11. Roberta was very upset by the news.
    _____

12. They were surprised by his behavior.
    _____

13. Her arm is broken in three places.
    _____

(44) Sequence of tenses

If the main verb of a sentence is in the past tense, put the verbs of the dependent clause in the past or past perfect tense.

Andrew *said* he *knew* Jessica very well.
Andrew *said* he *had known* Jessica very well.

Under this rule, the modal auxiliaries *can*, *may*, and *will* change to their respective past tense forms *could*, *might*, and *would* when they are part of the dependent clause.

Josh *said* that he *could swim* well.
Lynn *said* that she *would be* there by noon.

Choose the correct form of the verbs in parentheses.

1. He said he ___would___ be here. (will, would)

2. She says she _____ come back later. (might, may)

3. She thinks she _____ do it. (can, could)

4. I asked him whether we _____ smoke. (can, could)

5. Tom asked them whether he ___could___ smoke. (can, could)

6. He said that he _____ wait for us on the corner. (will, would)

7. I didn't know what the word _____ . (means, meant)

8. Our lawyer says she _____ a lot of work to do. (has, had)

9. The newspaper says it _____ rain tomorrow. (will, would)

10. He told me that they _____ a field at the time. (are crossing, were crossing)

11. Laura said she _____ away tomorrow. (was going, is going)

12. She said she _____ be here in a short time. (will, would)

13. I think he _____ twenty-five years old. (is, was)

14. I thought he _____ a good friend of mine. (is, was)

15. Mr. Chung says he _____ feel well. (doesn't, didn't)

16. She said her work _____ her busy. (keeps, kept)

17. The gardener said the flowers _____ . (have died, had died)

18. Her mother gave her the dress she _____ . (wants, wanted)

19. The doctor said she _____ die. (may, might)

20. She said her mother _____ a bad memory. (has, had)

21. Her mother said she always _____ the important things. (remembers, remembered)

44

(45) Direct and indirect speech

Examine the following two sentences carefully.

Eric said, "I am going away on Wednesday."
Eric said that he was going away on Wednesday.

The first sentence above is an example of direct speech because the words of the speaker are given exactly as spoken. The second sentence is an example of indirect speech because the words of the speaker are not given as spoken but are reported.

Note that when changing from direct to indirect speech, we change all the pronouns to agree with the sense of the new sentence. For example, the pronoun *I* in the first sentence was changed in the second sentence to *he*. Note also that in indirect speech, if the reporting verb is in the past tense, the rule of sequence of tenses must be followed. For example, *am going* was changed to *was going* in the second sentence.

Change the following from direct to indirect speech as in the example.

1. The doctor said, "Kenji is sick."
   <u>The doctor said that Kenji was sick.</u>

2. Tomiko said, "I know his name."

3. Nick said, "It is getting late."

4. He said, "We will have to hurry."

5. Watson said, "It looks like rain."

6. Monique said, "I have read that book."

7. Sue said, "I can call them by telephone."

8. Bijan said, "I have to go to the customs office."

9. The man said, "I need some money for soup and coffee."

(46) Indirect speech: questions

When direct questions are expressed in indirect speech, the question form is not retained. The auxilary verb is dropped or inverted with the subject of the question.

Rob asked, "Where does Clara live?"
Rob asked where Clara lived.

If a direct question does not begin with some question word like *when*, *where*, or *how*, it must be introduced by *if* when expressed in the indirect form.

Adela asked, "Does Ali live near the school?"
Adela asked if Ali lived near the school.

Change these sentences to the indirect speech form. Respond to *you* questions with *I*.

1. He said, "Where do you live?"
   He asked where I lived.

2. Ms. Cruz asked, "Do you like New York?"

3. She asked, "What time is it?"

4. Melanie asked, "Where is Busch Gardens?"

5. He asked, "Does Paolo sing well?"

6. The man asked, "How are you?"

7. My professor asked, "Where is Room 16?"

8. She asked, "Why do you smoke?"

9. The teacher asked, "Where is Andorra?"

10. She asked, "Is it going to rain?"

46

Indirect speech: commands

Orders or commands are expressed in indirect speech by use of an infinitive.

Mr. Murphy said to me, "Come back in ten minutes."
Mr. Murphy told me to come back in ten minutes.

Angela said to him, "Don't wait for the delivery."
Angela told him not to wait for the delivery.

Change the following statements to the indirect speech form.

1. She said to me, "Be quiet."

   She told me to be quiet.

2. They said to me, "Don't go."

   _____

3. I said to him, "Leave me alone."

   _____

4. You said to him, "Close the door."

   _____

5. She said to me, "Don't turn off the radio."

   _____

6. Anne said to David, "Sit down."

   _____

7. He said to her, "Think it over."

   _____

8. They said to me, "Come back later."

   _____

9. My father said to us, "Don't jump on the bed."

   _____

10. He said to her, "Don't come late."

    _____

11. My doctor said to him, "Take two aspirin and plenty of vitamin C."

    _____

12. She said to him, "Don't tell the answer."

    _____

(48) Causative form

When we wish to show that some action was performed, not by ourselves, but by somebody else at our instigation, we use the verb *to have* and the past participle of the main verb.

I shine my shoes.   I *have* my shoes *shined*.
He fixed his stereo.   He *had* his stereo *fixed*.

Change the following statements to the causative form.

1. I often cut my hair.
   <u>I often have my hair cut.</u>

2. He shines his shoes.
   _____

3. Sarah pressed her sweater.
   _____

4. Larry overhauled his old van.
   _____

5. I must fix my watch.
   _____

6. The front office mailed those letters.
   _____

7. We must paint our apartment.
   _____

8. The tenant must paint the apartment.
   _____

9. Ms. Jackson wants to clean her typewriter.
   _____

10. She is going to manicure her nails.
    _____

11. You want to resole your shoes.
    _____

12. I have filled the water tank.
    _____

13. My mother weeded her rose garden.
    _____

(49) Exclamatory form

When a noun is the principal word in an exclamatory sentence, begin the sentence with *what*.

What a beautiful day it is!   *What* a pretty flower!

To give emphasis to an adjective or an adverb in an exclamatory sentence, begin the sentence with *how*.

How well he swims!   *How* tall she is!

Change the following statements to the exclamatory form by using *what* or *how*.

1. She plays the piano very well.

   How well she plays the piano!

2. He is very handsome.

3. Her oldest daughter is a bright young lady.

4. They have learned English very quickly.

5. You have a beautiful new car.

6. Helen drives very well.

7. Ryan has grown very tall.

8. Paris is a charming city.

9. She has good taste.

10. They have a gorgeous home.

11. He is a lucky fellow.

(50) Emphatic form

Use *do*, *does*, and *did* in affirmative sentences to express emphasis or strong feeling.

I *do* feel tired.   We *did* finish our assignment.

Change the italicized verbs to the emphatic form.

1. He *mentioned* it to you.
   He did mention it to you.

2. She thinks he *knows* the song.

3. Fred didn't come, but he *telephoned*.

4. I *liked* it very much.

5. *Come* back later.

6. *Visit* us again sometime.

7. She *enjoys* her lessons.

8. We *did* these exercises.

9. I don't like movies, but I *like* the theater.

10. *Tell* us all about it.

11. He *tried* to please us.

12. We don't make much money, but we *have* a lot of fun.

13. I *know* a lot of Japanese phrases.

51 So

Use *so* after *think*, *believe*, *hope*, and *to be afraid* to respond to a question or comment upon a statement.

Is Mark coming to the party?	I don't think so.
She is too old for that work.	I believe so.
Will Sue be back soon?	I hope so.
Are we going to be late?	I'm afraid so.

Use *so* plus the verb in parentheses to answer or comment upon the following.

1. Do we have time to telephone them? (think)
   <u>I think so.</u>

2. Will Anthony be happy in that job? (not think)

3. The stores are open today, aren't they? (believe)

4. Perhaps he will give us the money. (not think)

5. It was Cortez who conquered Mexico, wasn't it? (believe)

6. He will probably fail his examination. (be afraid)

7. Can you finish the report by tomorrow? (believe)

8. Will Craig help you with this term paper? (hope)

9. Is it going to be sunny this afternoon? (hope)

10. Are we going to be late for class? (think)

11. Is that movie worth seeing? (believe)

12. Do they speak Spanish in Brazil? (not believe)

52 So, indeed, of course, naturally

Use *so* with a subject and an auxiliary verb to express surprise or agreeable astonishment.

Your computer is down. *So* it is!
His pen is leaking. *So* it is!
Your cigarette has gone out. *So* it has!

Use various other words to express emphatic agreement.

Betty has made great progress. *Indeed* she has!
Perhaps they are right. *Of course* they are!
He'll try to convince you of it. *Naturally* he will!

There in *there is/are* sentences is treated like a subject in this construction.

Complete these short responses. Answer *you* questions with *I* and *I* questions with *you*.

1. The window is wide open. So _____it is!_____

2. There is good weather ahead. Indeed _____

3. They have the same point of view. Of course _____

4. Tony must get more rest. Naturally _____

5. Mr. Kim has made good progress so far. Indeed _____

6. She is an excellent cook. Indeed _____

7. That ashtray is cracked. So _____

8. Anne is in the next room. So _____

9. Perhaps she owns a lot of property. Indeed _____

10. There are twelve tables empty. Of course _____

11. Your coffee is getting cold. So _____

12. This medicine can help you a lot. Of course _____

13. He can't leave without paying. Of course _____

14. They'll win first prize easily. Naturally _____

15. It's four o'clock already. So _____

16. Linda and Jim are great kids. Indeed _____

17. I'm doing better work now, don't you agree? Of course _____

18. It's very hot today, isn't it? Indeed _____

19. Doris has left already. So _____

53 Abbreviated clauses with *too, so*

Use *too* and *so* with a subject and an auxiliary verb to avoid the repetition of earlier words or phrases in an affirmative sentence.

She speaks English well, and he speaks English well.
She speaks English well, and *he does, too.*
She speaks English well, *and so does he.*

George went there, and Lawrence went there.
George went there, and *Lawrence did, too.*
George went there, and *so did Lawrence.*

Fill in the blanks with the correct auxiliary verb.

1. Natasha wants to study English, and she ____does____ , too.
2. You like San Francisco, and so _____ your wife.
3. Maria saw the movie, and so _____ I.
4. She is sick, and you _____ , too.
5. I will leave soon, and so _____ you.
6. We heard the explosion, and he _____ , too.
7. She has traveled all over the world, and he _____ , too.
8. They enjoyed the movie, and we _____ , too.
9. Teresa is bright, and so _____ her cousin, Matt.
10. Michiko will leave soon, and so _____ William.
11. I knew what they were doing, and Rita _____ , too.
12. Carla is going to study Portuguese, and so _____ her brother.
13. He has been to Europe, and I _____ , too.
14. Alice saw the accident, and so _____ I.
15. They are going to be late for class, and so _____ we.
16. You are very thoughtful, and so _____ your mother.
17. They want to give something, and I _____ , too.
18. The meat was salty, and the vegetables _____ , too.
19. My watch is slow, and so _____ Peter's.
20. He will help us, and Milton _____ , too.
21. I play soccer, and so _____ my roommate.

53

(54) Abbreviated clauses with *either, neither*

Use *either* and *neither* with a subject and an auxiliary verb to avoid the repetition of earlier words or phrases in a negative sentence.

He doesn't speak French, and she doesn't speak French.
He doesn't speak French, and she doesn't, either.
He doesn't speak French, and neither does she.

A. Shorten the following statements using *either*.

1. She doesn't study English, and he doesn't study English.
   She doesn't study English, and he doesn't, either.

2. He didn't go, and I didn't go.
   _____

3. He didn't study, and Marc didn't study.
   _____

4. She won't be there, and her sister won't be there.
   _____

5. Dolores hasn't heard the tape, and you haven't heard the tape.
   _____

6. You can't speak Latin, and Desmond can't speak Latin.
   _____

B. Shorten the following statements using *neither*.

1. Jane wasn't at the lesson, and her friend wasn't at the lesson.
   _____

2. Marta doesn't know them, and we don't know them.
   _____

3. Your watch doesn't have the right time, and my watch doesn't have the right time.
   _____

4. She hasn't seen him, and I haven't seen him.
   _____

5. Paula never rests, and Mindy never rests.
   _____

6. He wouldn't say that, and I wouldn't say that.
   _____

(55) *Supposed to*

Supposed to shows obligation on the part of the subject. The phrase is used only in the present and past tenses. Both tenses can be used in sentences with no time expression or with present or future time expressions.

They *are supposed to* be here.   They *were supposed to* be here.
The ship *is supposed to* arrive today. The ship *was supposed to* arrive today.

Only the past tense is used with past time expressions.

Joe *was supposed to* **go to Spain last year.**

Fill in the blanks with the correct form of *supposed to*. Use the past tense with past time expressions; use the present tense in all other cases.

1. They __are supposed to leave__ at ten o'clock. (leave)
2. Helen _____ here at five o'clock. (come)
3. You _____ the merchandise last week. (deliver)
4. Barry _____ me the book last month. (send)
5. She _____ this letter yesterday. (send)
6. I _____ a composition tonight. (write)
7. Mr. Robinson _____ here now. (be)
8. Everyone _____ that trip. (take)
9. The train _____ faster than the bus. (be)
10. Kathleen _____ here yesterday. (telephone)
11. Alice _____ a better student than Nan. (be)
12. We _____ a story about Washington in our English class. (read)
13. He _____ me tomorrow. (call)
14. I _____ at school at nine o'clock. (arrive)
15. The entire family _____ me at McDonald's. (meet)
16. The students _____ at least two hours on their homework. (spend)
17. He _____ her well. (know)
18. The company _____ this book last year. (publish)
19. I _____ early every day. (get up)
20. You _____ these chairs in the next room. (put)
21. The cook _____ dinner by eight o'clock. (prepare)
22. The children _____ to bed early tonight. (go)
23. This dictionary _____ the best. (be)

55

56 Used to

Used to **describes an action which continued for some period of time in the past but which is not taking place at the moment of speaking.**

She *used to* smoke. (She smoked for some time in the past, but now she does not smoke.)

I *used to* buy my clothes at Saks. (Now I buy them at another store.)

Change these sentences to the *used to* form.

1. She walked to work.

   She used to walk to work.

2. He worked here.

3. She came to class on time.

4. Monica was an industrious student.

5. He rode the subway to work.

6. Colette brought me flowers every day.

7. Mike played the trumpet very well.

8. He studied hard.

9. My adviser helped me very much.

10. I lived on Forty-sixth Street.

11. Her father went to that college.

12. I knew her well.

(57) To be used to

Students sometimes confuse *used to* with *to be used to*. *Used to* describes an action which continued for some time in the past. *To be used to* means "to be accustomed to"; the expression is always followed by a noun or a gerund.

I *used to* wear glasses. (I wore glasses at one time, but I do not wear them now.)

I *am used to* wearing glasses. (I am accustomed to wearing glasses.)

Fill in the blanks with *used to* or *to be used to*.

1. She ___used to___ play tennis well.
2. She ___is used to___ playing tennis with professionals.
3. You _____ smoke cigarettes.
4. You _____ smoking cigarettes.
5. Linda _____ wear glasses all the time.
6. Linda _____ wearing glasses all the time.
7. I _____ studying with a voice teacher.
8. I _____ study with a voice teacher.
9. He _____ live in New York.
10. He _____ living in New York.
11. We _____ having our English class early.
12. We _____ have our English class early.
13. Grace _____ work as a gardener.
14. Grace _____ working as a gardener.
15. I _____ have a large breakfast every morning.
16. I _____ having a large breakfast.
17. They _____ go to bed very early.
18. They _____ going to bed very early.
19. He _____ have his hair cut once a week.
20. He _____ having his hair cut by the same barber.
21. Ken _____ studying all night long.
22. Ken _____ study all night long.
23. She _____ clean the house.
24. She _____ cleaning the house.

(58) *Had better*

Had better refers to a present or future action which is necessary or advisable. It is followed by the simple form of the verb. It is usually contracted with the personal pronouns.

It is advisable that you see a doctor.   *You'd better* see a doctor.
It will be better if he studies.   *He'd better* study.

Form the negative by placing *not* after *better*.

You'd better leave now.   *You'd better not* leave now.
He'd better spend that money.   *He'd better not* spend that money.

Change the following to statements using *had better*. Use contractions with the personal pronouns.

1. It will be better if you come back later.
   You'd better come back later.

2. It will be better if he sees a doctor.

3. It will be better if Sue rests for a while.

4. It is advisable that you take private lessons.

5. It is advisable that they save a little money for a change.

6. It will be better if Peter doesn't mention this to anyone.

7. It is advisable that you give up smoking.

8. It will be better if she stops seeing him.

9. It is advisable that Dennis memorize these facts.

10. It is advisable that your lawyer call my lawyer.

11. However, it will be better if we don't give them too many details.

(59) *Would rather*

Would rather **indicates present or future preference. It is followed by the simple form of the verb. It is usually contracted with the personal pronouns.**

I prefer to study in the morning.   *I'd rather* study in the morning.
He prefers to see a movie.   *He'd rather* see a movie.

Form the negative by placing *not* **after** *rather.*

I'd rather study in the morning.   *I'd rather not* study in the morning.
He'd rather see a music video.   *He'd rather not* see a music video.

Change the following to statements using *would rather.* **Use contractions with the personal pronouns.**

1. I prefer to wait outside.
       I'd rather wait outside.

2. She prefers to come back later.

3. He prefers to watch TV.

4. They prefer to walk to school.

5. Dan prefers to do all his homework before he leaves school.

6. I prefer to stay home tonight and watch television.

7. Betty prefers to drive a big car.

8. We prefer to spend the summer at home instead of in the country.

9. He prefers not to speak to her about the matter again.

10. Marie prefers not to mention it to anyone.

11. She prefers to study in this class instead of the advanced class.

(60) *Can, could*

Can **has only two tenses, the present tense** *(can)* **and the past tense** *(could)*.
There is no infinitive. *Can* **may mean**

a. **ability**

        She can dance very well.

        I can meet you right after the lesson.

b. **possibility**

        One can catch cold easily in such weather.

        You can lose money fast in that kind of business.

c. **permission**

        I'll tell you when you can leave.

        No one can see him until Monday.

Change these sentences to the past tense.

1. He says he can meet us at noon.

   He said he could meet us at noon.

2. They think they can raise the money.

3. She thinks she can speak English as well as I.

4. He hopes he can get back here by five o'clock.

5. They feel that they can talk to you in confidence.

6. She insists she can convince him.

7. We think we can finish this book by June.

8. She says she can marry a doctor.

9. I can't get back before noon.

10. He can't leave this book here.

(61) *Should* after *if*

Use *should* in the *if* clause of a future possible conditional sentence to give emphasis to the verb or to suggest a possibility that is more remote than that described by the usual present tense verb.

> If Leo should come (i.e., "if by chance Leo comes" or "if it happens that Leo comes"), I will tell him about it.
> If it should rain while I am out, please close all the windows.

Notice that *should* is followed by the simple form of the verb.

Put *should* in the *if* clause of the following statements.

1. If Ruth happens to call, be sure to notify me.
   <u>If Ruth should call, be sure to notify me.</u>

2. If by chance you pass a mailbox, please mail this letter.

3. If it happens that the letter arrives, bring it to my office at once.

4. If by chance Dad hears about it, I won't be able to go.

5. If you happen to hear the rumor, don't believe it.

6. If by chance the electricity goes off, we will have to work in the dark.

7. If the weather happens to turn cold, we will be in an awful fix.

8. If the dog happens to bite her, she'll probably sue us.

9. If by chance a police officer happens to see you driving that way, you'll get a ticket.

10. If you happen to break the glass, you'll have to buy another.

11. If you happen to be free tomorrow, we'll go to a movie.

62 Difficult verbs:
raise, rise, set, sit

Raise **is a transitive verb. It is always followed by a direct object.**

George *raised* the window.
Mary *raised* her hand.

Rise **is an intransitive verb and is never followed by an object.**

The sun *rises* at seven o'clock.
Joe *rose* slowly to his feet.

Set **is a transitive verb, like** *raise,* **and is followed by a direct object.** *Sit,* **like** *rise,* **is intransitive.**

Mary *set* the book on the table.
Arthur always *sits* at this desk.

A. **Fill in the blanks with the correct form of** *raise* **or** *rise.*

1. Will you ____raise____ the curtain?
2. The sun _____ every day at six o'clock.
3. She _____ vegetables in her garden.
4. When the teacher asked the question, Norma _____ her hand.
5. The storm grew stronger, and the waves _____ .
6. The dough has already _____ .
7. Do you mind if I _____ the window?
8. Al got angry, _____ to his feet, and left the room.
9. That building is being _____ several feet.
10. They are trying to _____ money to build a new hospital.

B. **Fill in the blanks with the correct form of** *set* **or** *sit.*

1. Mother always ____sits____ at the head of the table.
2. Yesterday he _____ at another desk.
3. The Pilgrims _____ aside a day to give thanks.
4. Twelve people can _____ at this table.
5. Please _____ the table with the good china.
6. Daniela picked up the vase and _____ it on the table.
7. He is _____ in that chair now.
8. You can _____ in this seat near me.

(63) Difficult verbs: *lay, lie*

Lay, like *raise*, is a transitive verb. It is always followed by a direct object. The past form of *lay* is *laid*; the past participle is *laid*.

> She laid the books on the chair.
> They will lay the cornerstone tomorrow.

Lie like *rise*, is an intransitive verb and is never followed by a direct object. The past form of *lie* is *lay*; the past participle is *lain*.

> Your coat is lying on the floor.
> He lay down but could not rest.

A. Fill in the blanks with the correct form of *lay* or *lie*.

1. Yesterday he ____lay____ in the sun all day.
2. Her keys _____ on the kitchen counter.
3. You can _____ your coat on that chair.
4. The cat has _____ in that position all afternoon.
5. The carpet was _____ yesterday.
6. Your coat is _____ on the chair in the other room.
7. I thought I _____ it on the sofa in this room.
8. _____ on this sofa for a few minutes until you feel stronger.
9. Although he had _____ a cloth on the floor, the floor got stained.
10. The papers had been _____ in the rain for several hours.

B. Fill in the blanks with the correct form of the verbs in parentheses.

1. Help me ____raise____ the carpet. (raise, rise)
2. The hot-air balloon _____ silently in the east. (raised, rose)
3. The president _____ at dawn every morning. (raises, rises)
4. You can _____ the lamp on this table. (set, sit)
5. She _____ her coat over the back of the chair. (laid, lay)
6. Do you like to _____ in the sun? (lay, lie)
7. They are going to _____ the wages of their employees. (raise, rise)
8. Prices are _____ . (raising, rising)
9. The farmers _____ cattle and hogs. (raise, rise)
10. He has been _____ here asleep since two o'clock. (laying, lying)

(64) Participles

Participles in English have two forms, present and past (perfect). Both the present and past forms also have a passive voice. All participles are used as adjectives to modify nouns or pronouns.

Present active:	Seeing her approach, John ran away.
Present passive:	Being seen by her, he was embarrassed.
Perfect active:	Having seen her, he was glad to leave.
Perfect passive:	Having been seen by her, he was embarrassed.

Note that perfect participles indicate an action or situation earlier than that of the main verb of the sentence.

Change the italicized clauses to participial constructions.

1. *When I arrived there*, I found Frances sick.

   Arriving there, I found Frances sick.

2. *After she had finished the work*, she left.

3. *When I saw her*, I cried with joy.

4. *After he had spoken to her*, he was very happy.

5. *After he had been seen by her*, he had to admit everything.

6. *When we were leaving the party*, we ran into Joyce and Tom.

7. *After they had left here*, they went to another party.

8. The soldiers, *who were being forced to march*, pretended to be ill.

9. The men *who had been taken captive* finally escaped.

10. The day, *which had been a sad one*, finally ended.

(65) Gerunds 1

A gerund is a verb which ends in *ing* and is used as a noun. Certain verbs in English are always followed by gerunds rather than infinitives. Some of these verbs are *enjoy, mind, stop, avoid, consider, appreciate, finish, deny, admit, risk,* and *dislike.*

He apparently enjoys *studying* English.
Do you mind *closing* the window?
He has stopped *taking* English lessons.

Fill in the blanks with the gerund form of the verbs in parentheses.

1. I am considering ___taking___ a trip to Canada next summer. (take)
2. Ralph enjoys _____ with Mr. Fowler. (drive)
3. Mohammed stopped _____ to his English class. (go)
4. Do you mind _____ a few minutes in the hall? (wait)
5. We are considering _____ an automobile. (buy)
6. Did you enjoy _____ through Canada last summer? (travel)
7. Ask that representative whether she minds _____ back this afternoon. (come)
8. They are considering _____ the classes in the evening instead of the morning. (hold)
9. We will appreciate _____ an answer immediately. (receive)
10. They have finished _____ our apartment at last. (paint)
11. My mother was driving too fast and couldn't avoid _____ the other car. (hit)
12. Daniel denied _____ the change. (take)
13. You shouldn't risk _____ out if you have a cold. (go)
14. He admitted _____ the mistake after we questioned him for a long time. (make)
15. Ursula denied _____ the vase. (break)
16. Do you mind _____ down the radio? (turn)
17. I dislike _____ away from home for long periods of time. (go)
18. She has finished _____ for the day. (work)
19. You shouldn't risk _____ the roses too early. (plant)
20. They should finish _____ the apartment by eight o'clock. (clean)

(66) Gerunds 2

Since gerunds are used as nouns, they are used after prepositions in the same way that nouns are used. Do not make the mistake of using an infinitive instead of a gerund after prepositions.

We are both fond *of swimming.*   He insisted *on going* with us.

Fill in the blanks with the correct preposition and the gerund form of the verb in parentheses.

1. She is fond __of studying__ music. (study)

2. It is a question _____ several hours. (wait)

3. We are not interested _____ about his trip. (hear)

4. The woman had no excuse _____ to leave. (try)

5. I was afraid _____ my direction. (lose)

6. There was no chance _____ him there. (leave)

7. They were not successful _____ her. (find)

8. You will have no difficulty _____ him. (meet)

9. She needs more practice _____ English. (speak)

10. I am very fond _____ . (swim)

11. My son insisted _____ half the way. (drive)

12. We were looking forward _____ your friend from New York. (meet)

13. Nancy is getting tired _____ with computers. (work)

14. Tara was fearful _____ her balance. (lose)

15. There is little possibility _____ this work today. (finish)

16. He has no intention _____ it to anyone. (mention)

17. There is little chance _____ her today. (see)

18. She has no interest _____ that kind of work. (do)

19. His heart attack prevented him _____ with the work. (continue)

20. It is a question _____ the right person for the job. (find)

21. You can't really blame her _____ what she did. (do)

22. She seems to take pleasure _____ others. (help)

(67) Despite, in spite of

Despite and *in spite of* are prepositions and must be followed by nouns or noun equivalents.

Dr. Gonzalez came *despite* the horrible weather.
She came *in spite of* my warning.

If it is necessary to use a clause (a subject and a verb) after *despite* or *in spite of*, use *the fact that*.

Dr. Gonzalez came *despite the fact that* the weather was bad.
She came *in spite of the fact that* I warned her against it.

A. Fill in the blanks with *despite*.

1. He went for a walk _____ the rain.
2. Alma went out _____ the fact that it was stormy.
3. He studies hard _____ his illness.
4. Betty showed up early _____ her terrible cold.
5. _____ the fact that it was cold, we went to the ball game.

B. Fill in the blanks with *in spite of*.

1. She left _____ my warning.
2. _____ his illness, he does all the housework.
3. They failed _____ our good advice.
4. _____ the good advice we gave them, they didn't win the prize.
5. I'm going to stay home _____ the fine weather.

C. Complete these sentences. Use your own words.

1. They left despite _____.
2. He studied in spite of _____.
3. She arrived late despite _____.
4. I caught the bus despite the fact _____.
5. He went out without a hat or coat despite _____.
6. She went to the party despite the fact _____.
7. She became angry despite _____.
8. She was fired despite the fact _____.
9. He failed his examination despite the fact _____.

(68) *One*

Use *one* or *ones* to avoid repetition of some earlier word in a sentence. Generally, in such cases, *one* is used together with some adjective which serves to differentiate the second object from the first. Study these examples:

This fork is dirty; please bring me a clean *one*.
After looking over the new cars, I decided to keep my old *one* for another year.
Professional tapes are much better than amateur *ones*.

Substitute *one* or *ones* for the words in italics.

1. This knife is dull. Do you have a sharp *knife*?
   Do you have a sharp one?

2. The last lesson was difficult, but this *lesson* is easy.

3. This chair is very comfortable, but that *chair* is not.

4. They have two black cats and three white *cats*.

5. You were asking about a black notebook. Is this the *notebook* that you lost?

6. I like all games, but tennis and basketball are the *games* I like best.

7. We find that it is more fun to take several short trips than one long *trip*.

8. There were boats of all sizes in the bay, big *boats* and little *boats*.

9. We took pictures of almost everything, but the *pictures* we took of the bullfight turned out best.

10. This record is scratched; please give me a new *record*.

Adjective form of nouns

Give the adjective form of these nouns.

1. athlete	athletic	21. death	_____
2. thirst	_____	22. flower	_____
3. fool	_____	23. week	_____
4. quarrel	*Some*	24. month	_____
5. man	*manish*	25. taste	_____
6. child	*the*	26. summer	_____
7. greed	_____	27. winter	_____
8. wire	*wiry*	28. Denmark	_____
9. talent	_____	29. Ireland	_____
10. hour	_____	30. Scotland	_____
11. sun	_____	31. Sweden	*Swedish*
12. cloud	_____	32. Switzerland	_____
13. revolution *ary*	_____	33. Turkey	_____
14. hunger	_____	34. Spain	_____
15. day	_____	35. Mexico	_____
16. peace	_____	36. America	_____
17. need	_____	37. Canada	_____
18. dirt	_____	38. India	_____
19. culture	_____	39. Greece	_____
20. beauty	_____	40. Poland	_____

70 Noun form of adjectives

Give the noun form of these adjectives.

1. sad	_sadness_	21. desperate	_____
2. angry	_____	22. great	_____
3. deep	_____	23. beautiful	_____
4. happy	_____	24. rough	_____
5. high	_____	25. dead	_____
6. convenient	_____	26. loud	_____
7. ugly	_____	27. selfish	_____
8. possible	_____	28. cynical	_____
9. wide	_____	29. present	_____
10. sarcastic	_____	30. deceitful	_____
11. absent	_____	31. bitter	_____
12. dangerous	_____	32. sweet	_____
13. weak	_____	33. electric	_____
14. strong	_____	34. dry	_____
15. emphatic	_____	35. hot	_____
16. silent	_____	36. bashful	_____
17. intelligent	_____	37. proud	_____
18. generous	_____	38. dreary	_____
19. jealous	_____	39. true	_____
20. anxious	_____	40. clear	_____

(71) Until, as far as

Students sometimes confuse *until* **and** *as far as.* *Until* **is used only with reference to time** *(until tomorrow, until next week, until four o'clock).* As *far as* **is used with reference to distance, both physical and figurative** *(as far as page 10, as far as Seventy-ninth Street, as far as we could go, as far as I am concerned).*

Fill in the blanks with *until* **or** *as far as.*

1. We waited ___until___ ten o'clock.

2. The tour group walked _____ Rockefeller Center.

3. For tomorrow, study _____ page 76.

4. I have to stay here _____ Michelle calls.

5. We drove _____ Pittsburgh the first day.

6. He plans to stay there _____ February.

7. _____ I am concerned, you can do what you like.

8. I don't have to go to the doctor _____ next week.

9. We went only _____ exercise D in yesterday's lesson.

10. I guess we won't see you _____ next summer.

11. I won't see you, _____ I can tell, for some time.

12. She walked _____ the stream, then she turned back.

13. My family went _____ Los Angeles on their vacation.

14. Dan will be at the shore _____ late August.

15. The lab won't know _____ the results are in.

16. I told Johnny he could go _____ the sidewalk to play.

17. She told me to stay in bed _____ I felt stronger.

18. They went _____ the third lesson, and the bell rang.

19. Don't come in for dinner _____ I call you.

20. Try not to come _____ I have had my shower.

(72) Adverbs of time

While adverbs of time, such as *yesterday*, *last night*, *two days ago*, **go at the end of the sentence, adverbs of frequency, such as** *always, generally, seldom, usually, frequently, never, ever*, **go before the main verb.**

He *always studies* with me.   She *usually arrives* on time.

If an auxiliary verb is used, the adverb of frequency goes before the main verb.

She has *always loved* music.   He doesn't *usually eat* so late.

If the verb *to be* **is the only verb, adverbs of frequency follow it.**

They *are never* late.   We *were frequently* sick on that trip.

Place the adverb in parentheses in its correct position.

1. Rachel studies her lesson. (never)

   Rachel never studies her lesson.

2. I saw him on the street. (yesterday)

3. She comes to the lesson on time. (usually)

4. Luisa prepared her lesson well. (last night)

5. I see him on the street. (often)

6. My uncle reads *Time* magazine every week. (generally)

7. We go for a walk in the park on Sunday. (usually)

8. My friends and I went for a stroll in the park. (last Sunday)

9. She takes an early train. (never)

10. I drink milk. (seldom)

(73) *Still, anymore*

Still is an indefinite adverb of time meaning "even yet" or "even up to the present." It refers to some continuing action or state. Like adverbs of frequency, *still* precedes the main verb.

She is *still working* in that office.   They *still live* in the house they were born in.

The negative of *still* **is** *anymore. Anymore* **indicates that an action or state has been discontinued. It comes at the end of a sentence.**

She doesn't eat meat *anymore.*   I don't have a car *anymore.*

Fill in the blanks with *still* **or** *anymore.*

1. Marjan is ___still___ working in the bank.

2. Jimmy doesn't work here _____ .

3. They don't live in Miami _____ .

4. I am _____ studying English with Ann.

5. We never see you at the school dances _____ .

6. She is _____ the best student in the class.

7. I rarely see Carmen _____ .

8. He never comes to see us _____ .

9. We are _____ good friends, although I don't see them very often _____ .

10. My grandmother _____ likes to do her own baking.

11. Do they _____ have that crazy dog that barks at everyone constantly?

12. He doesn't believe they know him _____ .

13. He _____ thinks that he knows more English than anyone else.

14. They are _____ angry, but they are not fighting _____ .

15. We _____ haven't saved enough money, but we are _____ going to Europe.

16. Ted said he didn't love Joan _____ .

17. There are _____ some tickets left for tonight's show.

18. She _____ plays the piano, but she doesn't sing _____ .

19. Jack doesn't like school _____ , but he _____ goes.

(74) Else

Use *else* to form compounds with words that contain *some*, *any*, and *no* (*somebody else*, *anything else*, *nobody else*, *nowhere else*) **as a shorter and more convenient substitute for** *some other person*, *any other thing*, *no other person*, **and so on.**

Did you go *anywhere else* (i.e., any other place) after the dance?
Nobody else (i.e., no other person) would believe him.

Else **is also compounded with the question words** *what*, *where*, *how*, **and** *who* **to give the meaning of "other" or "in addition."**

Where *else* did you go?	How *else* could I tell him?
What *else* does she want?	Who *else* came to the party?

Substitute the correct expression with *else* **for the words in italics. Although** *someone else* **and** *no one else* **are used, use the words with** *body* **in this exercise.**

1. Did they go *any other place*?

   <u>Did they go anywhere else?</u>

2. *No other person* helped him with the work.

   _____

3. You must ask *some other person* about it.

   _____

4. *What other person* knows the combination?

   _____

5. They have never sold that merchandise *in any other place*.

   _____

6. Did you see *any other thing* that you liked?

   _____

7. Let's do *some other thing* tonight besides watch television.

   _____

8. I didn't tell *any other person* about it.

   _____

9. *In what other way* can I paint the room?

   _____

(75) Question words with *ever*

Add *ever* to the words *what, who, where, when,* and *which* to form the compounds *whatever, whoever, wherever, whenever,* and *whichever*. The *ever* adds emphasis to these words and supplies the additional meaning of "regardless of (the situation)" or "no matter what."

Whoever (i.e., anyone, no matter who) gets there first will win a prize.

Wherever she goes (i.e., regardless of where she goes), everyone likes her.

Whenever I go out with him (i.e., no matter when I go out with him), I have a good time.

Fill in the blanks with *whatever, whoever, wherever, whenever,* or *whichever*.

1. We saw flowers __wherever__ we went.

2. _____ goes to California will find a beautiful climate.

3. He said we could come _____ we wanted.

4. The doctor says he can eat _____ he wants.

5. She said we could bring _____ we wanted.

6. I'll go with you _____ you are ready.

7. Sue will be happy with _____ she gets.

8. _____ studies English always has difficulty with the pronunciation.

9. I will follow him _____ he goes.

10. _____ she comes, she always brings us a present.

11. We were free to go _____ we chose.

12. He said, "Come again _____ you like."

13. Hang up your coat _____ you can find a hook for it.

14. You can take _____ one you want, and you can bring it back _____ you wish.

15. I've always enjoyed myself _____ I went there.

16. The doctor says Joe can have an appointment _____ he wants.

17. _____ she does one of these exercises, she makes at least ten mistakes.

18. _____ has my pen, please return it immediately!

19. _____ she cooks always turns out to have the same taste.

(76) Expressions of quantity

Much and *little* are used with noncount nouns, which have no plural form.
Many and *few* are used with plural count nouns.
A lot of is used interchangeably with *much* and *many*. *A lot of* is more commonly used than *much* or *many*.

much sugar	much rain	a lot of paper
little sugar	little rain	
many books	many trees	a lot of pages
few books	few trees	

Fill in the blanks with the correct adjective in parentheses.

1. He smokes __a lot of__ cigarettes. (much, a lot of)

2. There are _____ large factories in that town. (much, many)

3. There isn't _____ honey left in the jar. (many, much)

4. There is _____ grass in that meadow. (many, a lot of)

5. Do you have a _____ extra pencils? (few, little)

6. We had _____ money with us. (few, little)

7. I need a _____ more time to finish. (few, little)

8. She made _____ mistakes. (few, little)

9. We haven't heard _____ news lately. (many, much)

10. A _____ friends are coming over tonight. (few, little)

11. Janie spends too _____ time on her homework. (few, little)

12. There are _____ bags in the hallway. (a lot of, much)

13. How _____ pounds did you lose? (much, many)

14. How _____ weight did you lose? (much, many)

15. We sat there for _____ hours. (much, many)

16. There is _____ snow on the ground. (a lot of, many)

17. There are _____ elegant restaurants in this town. (many, little)

18. There isn't _____ ink in this pen. (few, much)

19. How _____ languages can you speak? (much, many)

20. How _____ time do you have to spend with us? (much, many)

77 General review

Fill in the blanks with the correct word in parentheses.

1. He is an old friend of ___hers___ . (she, her, hers)
2. I bought this pencil at _____ store. (Nicks, Nick's)
3. Sheep _____ timid animals. (is, are)
4. Sally sat directly in front of Bill and _____ . (I, me)
5. We are much stronger than _____ in all phases of athletics. (they, them)
6. There _____ down the street. (comes Phil, Phil comes)
7. They knew all about my job and _____ . (I, me)
8. The boys will hurt _____ if they are not careful. (himself, themselves)
9. She seemed like _____ thoroughly honest person. (a, an)
10. Mike Lopez is _____ old friend of mine. (a, an)
11. She drove at a speed of eighty miles _____ hour. (a, an)
12. If you have finished with those magazines, why don't you throw _____? (away them, them away)
13. Rosemary asked me to call _____ at exactly two o'clock. (up her, her up)
14. If you are looking for Anita, there _____ down the street now. (comes she, she comes)
15. We told Barry and _____ all about it. (they, them)
16. What _____ beautiful day! (a, an)
17. She caught _____ terrible cold last winter. (a, the)
18. Roy is _____ excellent student. (a, an)
19. The technician has already put _____ program away. (she, her)
20. The teacher gave _____ his book. (I, me)
21. She _____ cooked the dinner. (herself, by herself)
22. We _____ are to blame. (ourselves, for ourselves)
23. This book is mine, and that one is _____ . (your, yours)
24. My grandparents bought me _____ own car. (my, mine)

(78) Position of prepositions 1

In everyday English conversation, avoid beginning any direct question with a preposition. Instead, begin the question with the object of the preposition and shift the preposition to the end of the sentence.

What is he looking *for*?
What state does she come *from*?

Supply the appropriate preposition to complete each of these questions.

1. What are they talking __about__?
2. What are you thinking _____?
3. What country was he born _____?
4. Whom (who) do you wish to speak _____?
5. What kind of car are you looking _____?
6. Whom (who) does this book belong _____?
7. What are they going to use the money _____?
8. Which restaurant do you want to eat _____?
9. Which dealer did you buy your van _____?
10. Whom (who) was the book written _____?
11. Which hotel did he go _____?
12. Whom (who) did they sell their house _____?
13. Which paintings do you want to look _____?
14. What is the guide pointing _____?
15. Which room do you have your lesson _____?
16. Where did all this loose change come _____?
17. What are you smiling _____?
18. Who are you looking _____?
19. Where did you take this book _____?
20. Where do you come _____?

(79) Position of prepositions 2

If a sentence contains a relative pronoun which is the object of a preposition, this preposition is generally shifted to the end of the sentence or clause. Notice, moreover, that in sentences of this type, we frequently drop the relative pronoun altogether.

This is the book (that) I was talking about.
She is the clerk (that) I spoke to yesterday.

Change these sentences by dropping the relative pronoun and shifting the preposition.

1. This is the movie about which everyone is talking.

   This is the movie everyone is talking about.

2. The woman to whom you were speaking is my teacher.

3. That is the store in which I lost my purse.

4. She is the kind of representative from whom it is difficult to get away.

5. The adviser to whom you should speak is Dr. Kojima.

6. It is a subject on which we will never agree.

7. The thing about which they were arguing was really of little importance.

8. It is a place in which you will feel at home.

9. It was Charles for whom I had to wait so long.

10. It was Jack from whom he borrowed the money.

11. The room in which we study is on the second floor.

12. This is the street on which they live.

80 Review: special difficulties 1

Rob, steal
One steals an object, but one robs a person or thing.
They stole money from the bank's safe. place
They robbed the bank.

Some, somewhat
Some **is an adjective and must modify a noun or pronoun;** *somewhat* **is an adverb and is used to modify an adjective or another adverb.**
He has some money and some food to contribute.
Beatrice feels somewhat better after her trip.

In, into
In **suggests position within a certain space;** *into* **suggests action toward a certain point.**
The money is in the drawer.
He threw the money into the drawer.

Affect, effect, advise, advice
Affect **and** *advise* **are verbs;** *effect* **and** *advice* **are nouns.**
The wine affected Harold quickly.
He soon felt the effects of the wine.
She advised me to take the course.
I intend to follow her advice.

Fill in the blanks with the correct word in parentheses.

1. They arrived __somewhat__ early. (some, somewhat)

2. The _____ of his efforts was obvious. (effect, affect)

3. The _____ of the teacher's discipline were evident. (effects, affects)

4. What do you _____ me to do? (advice, advise)

5. She walked right _____ their trap. (in, into)

6. The thief _____ my watch. (stole, robbed)

7. This coffee seems _____ better than usual. (some, somewhat)

8. She was obviously _____ by the bad news. (effected, affected)

9. I should have taken your _____ . (advise, advice)

10. The coffee was _____ bitter. (some, somewhat)

11. Who _____ my new pencil? (stole, robbed)

12. The man claimed that someone had _____ him. (stolen, robbed)

13. I keep my money _____ a safe. (in, into)

(81) Review: special difficulties 2

Beside, besides
Beside means "alongside of"; *besides* means "in addition to."

John sits beside me in class.
Two boys besides John took the trip.

Teach, learn
Learn means "to gain knowledge"; it is impossible to "learn" another person. *Teach* means "to instruct someone else."

I learned French in high school.   Rose taught me how to swim.

Infinitives without *to*
Note that infinitives without *to* **are used after the verbs** *let, make, hear, see,* **and** *feel.*

He let me borrow his bicycle.   She made us wait an hour.

Negative openings
Note that if an English sentence begins with a negative word, an auxiliary verb or some form of *to be* **must precede the subject, as in interrogative sentences.**

Never have I heard such music.   Not once did he mention your name.

Fill in the blanks with the correct word in parentheses.

1. Two other children ___besides___ Mary left for camp. (beside, besides)

2. Who _____ you how to speak English? (taught, learned)

3. Never _____ seen him so happy. (I have, have I)

4. I put my homework on the seat _____ me. (beside, besides)

5. Melanie is going to _____ us how to knit. (learn, teach)

6. She sits _____ me in class. (beside, besides)

7. He was _____ French by a good teacher. (taught, learned)

8. They saw us _____ the dog. (to pet, pet)

9. Not once _____ taxes. (he mentioned, did he mention)

10. The doctor made us _____ two hours. (to wait, wait)

11. Nowhere _____ find a more generous person. (you could, could you)

12. I asked him _____ with us. (to go, go)

13. Never have we _____ such a sight! (see, seen)

82 Review: special difficulties 3

No, not

No is an adjective and is used to modify nouns.

He has *no* money and *no* friends.

Not is an adverb and is used

   a. to modify verbs
   b. before the adjectives *much, many, any, enough*
   c. before any article or numeral used to modify a noun
      He does *not* speak English well.
      Not many people came to the meeting.
      Not a person spoke; *not* one word of protest was heard.

Spill, pour

Spill suggests some unintentional or accidental action; *pour*, some intentional action.

She carelessly *spilled* the milk on the floor.
Joan carefully *poured* the tea into the cup.

Win, beat

One wins a game, but one beats or defeats an opponent.

Alice *won* the game of chess easily.
Alice easily *beat* Roger at chess.

===

Fill in the blanks with the correct word in parentheses.

1. Ben ___beat___ me in a game of poker. (won, beat)
2. There are _____ boys in that class. (no, not)
3. He _____ the game of chess. (won, beat)
4. There are _____ many flowers in that vase. (no, not)
5. The baby _____ cereal all over the floor. (spilled, poured)
6. She _____ the milk in the glass. (spilled, poured)
7. _____ one girl wanted to dance with him. (No, Not)
8. Dennis carefully _____ the cream into the pitcher. (spilled, poured)
9. Who _____ the baseball game? (won, beat)
10. I told him to _____ some of the water out of the glass. (spill, pour)
11. _____ sane person would say such a thing. (No, Not)
12. _____ a single member spoke during that meeting. (No, Not)

Fill in the articles where needed. If no article is needed, leave a blank.

1. ___The___ chair on which you are sitting is not comfortable.

2. _____ fire which destroyed _____ building started on _____ tenth floor.

3. I bought _____ new hat yesterday. It has _____ wide brim and _____ narrow band. _____ man who sold it to me said it was _____ new style from _____ Paris.

4. The boy took _____ his book and put it into _____ his briefcase.

5. They enjoyed _____ speech of _____ Dr. Lao, who spoke on _____ situation in Vietnam.

6. We all had _____ good time at _____ dance last night.

7. _____ price of _____ gold is rising, but _____ price of _____ silver is falling.

8. Much of _____ silver which we use in _____ United States comes from _____ Montana.

9. _____ drinking water often varies in taste, according to locality. _____ drinking water in New York City is quite good.

10. There are _____ several new magazines on _____ table in _____ hall.

11. Let us take _____ Broadway bus to _____ 110th Street and then change to _____ Fifth Avenue bus and go up _____ Riverside Drive.

12. We often go to _____ Central Park and watch _____ animals in _____ zoo.

13. Please open _____ windows. _____ air in this room is no good.

14. They plan to visit _____ Russia this summer. I understand _____ Russian language is difficult to learn.

15. Mr. and Mrs. Nomura are now traveling in _____ South America. They plan to visit _____ Venezuela, _____ Colombia, _____ Peru, and _____ Argentina.

16. They will arrive in _____ Netherlands at _____ noon.

17. _____ noon train from _____ Washington comes in on _____ track 10.

18. _____ weather today is very warm.

Use the comma to separate words, phrases, or clauses in a series.

We need books, pencils, chairs, and desks.
We played tennis, took long walks, and went swimming.

Use the comma to set off items in dates, addresses, and geographical names.

He lives in Chicago, Illinois.
It happened on Tuesday, November 27, 1981.

Use the comma to set off parenthetical expressions and words in direct address. Also use the comma to set off all appositives.

He was, to be sure, an excellent diplomat.
And so, my friends, you can see the results.
Jack, our butcher, was hurt recently.

Punctuate these sentences.

1. We study history mathematics geography and reading.

2. Sue Bielski the mechanic repaired our car and also fixed our refrigerator.

3. He was of course more to be pitied than censured.

4. Mike Madison the head of the company will see you on Sunday.

5. The governor in the first place did not pardon the murderer.

6. He was born in Scranton Pennsylvania on March 23 1980, and he has lived there ever since.

7. We cannot after all live forever.

8. By the way do you remember Mrs. Jackson's telephone number?

9. Sue Brown Henry's cousin is visiting him at the latter's camp in Stroudsburg Pennsylvania.

10. Where were you Miss Lyons on the morning of June 26 1983?

11. The old Amos Building a famous landmark of the town was recently torn down. As a matter of fact it was torn down on February 12 Lincoln's Birthday.

12. The most popular summer sports are tennis swimming and hiking.

13. Yesterday I met three former schoolmates Tom Beck Ruth Sanchez and Randy Owens.

14. The last time I saw them was on August 3 1982.

85 Punctuation: the comma 2

Use the comma to set off any long adverbial clause which precedes a main clause. Also set off any such clause which occurs out of its normal position and thus interrupts the normal order of the sentence.

When the wind began to blow hard, we ran for shelter.
We might, if the rain continues much longer, have to postpone our trip.

but

We might have to postpone our trip if the rain continues much longer.

Use the comma to set off all absolute phrases. An absolute phrase consists of a noun and a participle used together in a construction independent of the rest of the sentence.

The rain having stopped, we decided to continue our trip.

Punctuate these sentences.

1. If it rains we may have to postpone our trip.
2. I may if the weather is bad cancel the class trip.
3. We may have to postpone our trip if it rains.
4. When he protested so vigorously we withdrew our proposal.
5. Because he was so widely read he had a comprehensive grasp of the entire subject.
6. Our work being over for the day we closed shop and went home.
7. Because he had been ill he asked to be excused from all assignments.
8. If Monica wanted she could be a very good student.
9. Yoshiko having gotten a visa bought the airline ticket.
10. He never studied any foreign language when he was in high school.
11. When he was in high school he never studied any foreign language.
12. He never when he was in high school studied any foreign language.
13. Although she was a skilled engineer she did not know the first thing about road building.
14. Natasha was as was easily seen from her speech a woman of strong opinions.

(86) Punctuation: the comma 3

Use the comma to set off any nonrestrictive clause. A nonrestrictive clause is one which is not necessary to the meaning or identification of the word which it modifies. It is, in other words, a clause which might actually be set off in parentheses.

Use no punctuation at all with restrictive clauses.

Nonrestrictive:	Dr. Matany, *who is very skillful*, has a big practice.
Restrictive:	Any doctor *who is very skillful* has a big practice.
Nonrestrictive:	Whittier, *where we met*, was then a pretty little town.
Restrictive:	The place *where we met* was a pretty little town.

Punctuate these sentences.

1. Barbara who is quite smart deserves to pass.

2. Any student who is lazy does not deserve to pass.

3. Any girl who has brown hair will be all right for the part of the heroine.

4. Angela who has brown hair was selected for the part of the heroine.

5. Daniel's hands feet and face which were covered with mud were washed by Mother.

6. Any passenger who enters the engine room does so at his or her own risk.

7. The person who said that is mistaken.

8. Eva who told the story was obviously misinformed.

9. Wednesday when my brother is usually out of town will be a good day to call.

10. Ms. Rubio who was in the real estate business decided to promote Glen Acres which was formerly a swamp.

11. The fellow who was laughing was clearly the perpetrator of the joke.

12. His great love for nature which he acquired during his childhood showed itself in his curiosity about any bird which flew through his garden.

13. The profit which you can expect on so cheap an article is very small.

14. We heard a noise that resembled the cry of an injured animal.

15. The George Washington Bridge which spans the Hudson River has been very successful financially.

16. Kyle unlike his brother Josh has brown hair blue eyes and a light complexion.

87 Punctuation:
the comma and semicolon

Use a comma to separate two independent clauses joined by *or*, *and*, **or** *but* **unless the clauses are very short.**

In the North there are many wheat fields, but in the South cotton fields predominate.
We had great trouble in reaching him, but at last he answered.

If such clauses are not connected by *or*, *and*, **or** *but* **yet are related in meaning, they can be joined by a semicolon.**

In the North there are many wheat fields; in the South cotton fields predominate.
We had great trouble in reaching him; at last, however, he answered.

Punctuate these sentences.

1. Chicago is my favorite city but Philadelphia offers more advantages.
2. Fools need advice only wise men profit by it.
3. The general manager will talk to you soon and will give you the information.
4. Alec is a very good automobile mechanic and his prices are low.
5. I had the passport for a week but then finally I returned it.
6. She kept the book for a long time but she finally returned it.
7. Bill had the ring then he gave it to Joe.
8. There were six ambassadors and their entrance was truly magnificent.
9. Marcia didn't go but Colleen did.
10. Mary was highly pleased with the results therefore she showed her pleasure and gave us all a quarter.
11. Lou was pleased with the results but Mr. Martin obviously wasn't.
12. Cowards die many times but a brave man dies but once.
13. Marianne was cautious but Henry bet on the black horse and won more than twenty dollars.
14. Tom plays the bass and Dennis plays the acoustic guitar.
15. I like Trivial Pursuit my sister likes Monopoly.
16. He was tattered and dirty but he ate like a gentleman.
17. My brother or my mother will help you and will gladly show you the way.

88 Review: punctuation

Punctuate the following statements.

1. The changes which we are planning will soon be completed.

2. Jenny and Alice came into the room looked around whispered to each other and then walked out.

3. Williams store which sells many fancy groceries was recently repainted and as a consequence it now looks very nice.

4. I am sure Sophie said Henry you will like our new summer place which was built by the local company.

5. Of course Father its a pity said Ellen that people dont appreciate the excellent work that you have done here.

6. We drove from Harrisburg Pa to Albany which is the capital of New York State.

7. Mary and Ellen stopped and watched Henry and Joseph running and jumping.

8. We Mary Ethel and I considered going but later we changed our minds and decided to stay at home and rest.

9. The woman whom we saw yesterday was Don Grays sister Terry Nelson who is a psychologist.

10. Saturday Jan 16 was the coldest day that we had but the next day seemed even colder to me.

11. Everyone got into the van we started out and soon we were on the freeway.

12. At eleven Rex adjourned the meeting no decision having been reached by that time.

13. I believe said the visitor that Mr Davis should be notified at once yet we all realize that the duty is not a pleasant one.

14. Strangely enough Heather and Jennifer came into the room looked at the table sat down and began to read.

15. She is very intelligent but the lack of a diploma would prevent her from entering any college even one of low standards.

(89) Spelling rules

Students will find the four simple rules of spelling which follow very helpful. They should try to memorize them.

1. A word ending in silent *e* generally drops the *e* before a suffix beginning with a vowel and retains it before a suffix beginning with a consonant. Example:

   move–movable   like–likable   move–movement   like–likely

   After *c* or *g*, if the suffix begins with *a* or *o*, the *e* is retained in order to keep the soft sound of *c* or *g*. Examples:

   notice–noticeable   change–changeable   advantage–advantageous

2. In words with *ie* or *ei*, use *i* before *e*, except after *c*, when the sound is "ee."

   believe   fierce   receive   conceive   grief   cashier
   Exceptions: neither   either   seize   financier   weird   leisure

3. A noun ending in *y* preceded by a consonant takes the ending *ies* in the plural. A verb ending in *y* preceded by a consonant forms its present tense, third person singular, in *ies*. If the terminal *y* in such words is preceded by a vowel, then only an *s* is added.

   lady–ladies   army–armies   marry–marries   fly–flies   valley–valleys
   chimney–chimneys   enjoy–enjoys   delay–delays

4. In words of one syllable or words accented on the last syllable which end in a single consonant preceded by a single vowel, double the consonant before a suffix beginning with a vowel.

   drop–dropped   occur–occurring   confer–conferring   stop–stopping
   open–opened   offer–offered   feel–feeling

Practice the spelling of these troublesome words.

worshiping	daisies	receive	chief	controlled
occurrence	preferred	offered	seize	trapped
equipped	centuries	occurring	relieve	forties
equipment	useful	benefited	omitted	excitable
noticeable	usable	permitting	armies	famous
deceive	incurable	forgetting	turkeys	piece
feeling	adorable	monkeys	hopeful	beginning
conceive	lovable	canceled	shriek	leisure
conceivable	outrageous	dries	offering	neither
begging	traceable	loveless	offered	shield
financier	singeing	priest	employs	

90 Mark Twain and the Game Warden

Because Mark Twain was both famous and popular in his day, there are many, many stories about him, particularly many humorous stories.

One day Mark Twain was fishing. A stranger came along.

"Good morning!" said the stranger.

"Good morning," said Twain. "It's a fine day, isn't it?"

"An excellent day," said the stranger. "Are you catching any fish?"

"The fishing is very good here. I caught three trout here yesterday in about an hour."

"Is that so?" said the stranger.

"Yes, and I'm very fond of trout."

"By the way," said the stranger, "do you happen to know who I am?"

"No, I haven't the remotest idea," said Mark Twain.

"Well, I'm the game warden of this county," said the stranger. "And trout are out of season."

Twain paused a moment. Then he said, "By the way, do you know who I am?"

"No, I don't."

"Well, I'm the biggest liar in this county."

Write the letter of the correct answer in the blank.

1. Mark Twain was _____ .

   a. popular   b. unpopular

2. When the stranger came along, Mark Twain was _____ .

   a. working   b. fishing

3. The stranger asked Twain if he was _____ .

   a. working   b. fishing

4. Twain said he had caught _____ fish.

   a. thirteen   b. three

5. Twain was very fond of _____ .

   a. trout   b. bass

6. The stranger was a _____ .

   a. police officer   b. game warden

7. Trout were _____ .

   a. out of season   b. in season

8. Twain said he was _____ .

   a. an honest man   b. a liar

91 Mark Twain and the Train Ticket

Mark Twain was a famous American writer of novels and short stories. He was also famous in his day as a lecturer and humorist. He liked to tell funny stories, and he also liked to play jokes on his friends. One day, a friend of his lost his wallet and asked Twain to pay his railroad fare for him.

Twain said, "I'm sorry, but it happens that I have very little money with me. I don't have enough money to pay both your fare and my own."

The friend was very sad.

"However," said Twain, "you can get on the train with me and, when the conductor comes through the train to collect the tickets, you can hide under my seat."

The friend had no other alternative, so he finally agreed to this plan. Later, however, when the conductor came through the train, Twain gave him two tickets, one for himself and one for his friend under the seat.

Then in a loud voice, so that everybody in the train could hear him easily, Twain explained, "My friend here is a very strange fellow. When he rides on a train, he doesn't like to sit on the seat. He prefers to lie on the floor under the seat."

Of course, everybody then looked at the poor fellow under the seat and laughed at him loudly.

===

Write the letter of the correct answer in the blank.

1. Mark Twain's friend lost his _____ .
   - a. ticket
   - b. money

2. He asked Twain to _____ .
   - a. buy his ticket
   - b. give him money

3. Twain said that he _____ enough money.
   - a. didn't have
   - b. had

4. Twain suggested that the man _____ the seat.
   - a. sit on
   - b. hide under

5. Twain's friend finally _____ .
   - a. disagreed
   - b. agreed

6. Twain gave the conductor _____ .
   - a. one ticket
   - b. two tickets

7. Twain spoke to the conductor in a _____ voice.
   - a. loud
   - b. soft

92 The Pied Piper of Hamelin

Everyone knows the story "The Pied Piper of Hamelin." The story concerns the town of Hamelin, which was visited by a great number of rats many centuries ago. The people of the town tried everything to get rid of the rats but without success. At last, a strange man, dressed in a suit of many colors, visited the town and offered to get rid of all the rats—but at a high price. The people agreed gladly. The man then took out his flute, played some strange music, and walked slowly from the town with all the rats following him. A few days later, he returned for his money, but the people did not want to pay him. The rats were all gone now; he had done very little work; and his price was too high. The piper took out his flute again, played more strange music, and this time all the children of the village followed him out of the city, never to return.

Write the letter of the correct answer in the blank.

1. This story took place _____ .
   a. recently   b. many centuries ago

2. The town was visited by a great number of _____ .
   a. rats   b. flies

3. The people tried to get rid of the rats _____ success.
   a. with   b. without

4. A _____ offered to get rid of the rats.
   a. woman   b. man

5. He asked a _____ price.
   a. high   b. low

6. The people _____ his offer.
   a. refused   b. agreed to

7. The rats _____ the music of the flute.
   a. followed   b. ran away from

8. After the rats were gone, the people _____ to pay the man.
   a. agreed   b. refused

9. The piper took their _____ .
   a. money   b. children

10. The children _____ returned.
    a. never   b. soon

(93) The Three Wishes

Long ago, there lived a couple who had a dairy farm. They were poor and spent much of their time wishing for things they did not have.

Often the man would say, "I wish I were handsome," or "I wish I had more cows."

Frequently the woman would say, "I wish I were wealthy," or "I wish I were a beautiful princess."

One day, some fairies heard their wishes and decided to conduct an experiment. They went to the couple and granted them three wishes. Whatever they wished would truly be granted.

The couple talked a long time over what they should wish for. But after a while they became hungry, and from force of habit the woman suddenly said, "I wish I had some sausages to eat."

Immediately her market basket was full of sausages.

Then a heated argument began because the husband said that his wife had wasted one of their valuable wishes on such a cheap thing as sausages. The argument grew hotter, and finally in anger the wife said, "I wish these sausages were hanging from your nose!"

Of course the sausages immediately flew to the poor man's nose and stayed there. Nor could they be removed. Now, there was only one thing the poor woman could do. She really loved her husband, and so she had to spend their third wish in removing the sausages from his nose. Thus, except for a few sausages, they had nothing to show for their three wishes.

Write the letter of the correct answer in the blank.

1. The woman spent her time _____ .

    a. working   b. wishing

2. The fairies gave her _____ wishes.

    a. three   b. four

3. The woman became _____ .

    a. sleepy   b. hungry

4. She wished for _____ .

    a. a bed   b. some sausages

5. Then she became _____ .

    a. angry   b. happy

6. She wished the sausages were on _____ .

    a. her husband's nose b. the plate

7. The sausages flew to _____ .

    a. the plate   b. her husband's nose

94 The Indian Prince

Once upon a time, there was a young prince in India who had been ill for some time. As a result of his illness, he developed some rather strange ideas. For example, he became convinced that he was a cow. Since it was the practice in his religion to sacrifice cows, he then insisted on being sacrificed like all other cows. Many famous doctors were called in to treat him, but none of them was able to help him. Finally, after all the others had failed, an old village doctor was called. The old doctor, after considering the case carefully, began to pretend that he was the village priest and that he had become to sacrifice the prince. He took out a long knife and began to feel the prince's arms and legs in order to find the best place to cut him. Then he suddenly stopped.

"I cannot cut this animal to offer it as sacrifice to the gods," he said. "This animal is much too thin and weak to sacrifice. It would be an insult to offer such a poor specimen."

The prince was naturally very much disturbed. "But you must," he insisted.

"Surely you agree with me, Your Highness," persisted the old doctor.

"If I must get fatter, then I shall do so," the prince finally agreed. He therefore began to eat and drink large quantities of food. He ate and ate, and as the weeks passed, he became much fatter. But at the same time, his strength also increased, and his health improved. in fact, he soon felt so much better that he forgot all about being a cow.

Write the letter of the correct answer in the blank.

1. The story is about _____ prince.

   a. an Indian   b. a French

2. The prince had been sick for a _____ time.

   a. long   b. short

3. He thought he was a _____ .

   a. lion   b. cow

4. In his religion, it was the practice to _____ cows.

   a. eat   b. sacrifice

5. The doctor pretended that he was a _____ .

   a. soldier   b. priest

6. The doctor _____ to make the sacrifice.

   a. refused   b. agreed

(95) Three Men and a Train

Three men stood drinking at a bar near a railroad station. They were waiting for a train and had, therefore, asked the porter to inform them when the train arrived. A short time later, the porter appeared in the doorway of the bar to tell them that the train was just coming in.

"Ah!" said the men. "We have time for just one more drink." They then all took another drink and ran out, but they missed the train.

They went back to the bar in order to await the arrival of the next train. They continued drinking. An hour later, the second train arrived, and the same thing happened. They missed the train again.

Two hours later, the porter appeared to say that the third and last train was just coming in. Again the men waited long enough to have one more drink, and then they all ran out. Two of the men, being tall, could run fairly fast. They caught the train. But the third man, who was short, again missed the train. Very slowly, he walked back to the bar and began drinking again.

"By the way," the bartender said to him after a while, "where are your two friends going?"

"I don't know where they're going," the man said. "They just came down to the station to see me off."

Write the letter of the correct answer in the blank.

1. The men were waiting for a _____ .
   a. train   b. plane

2. They were waiting in a _____ .
   a. station   b. bar

3. When they heard that the train was coming, they said that they _____ .
   a. had to go   b. had time for another drink

4. They _____ the first train.
   a. caught   b. missed

5. When they heard that the second train was coming, they said that they _____ .
   a. had time for another drink b. had to go

6. They _____ the second train.
   a. missed   b. caught

7. When the third train came, they _____ another drink.
   a. didn't have   b. had

Robert Bruce and the Spider

Robert Bruce was a famous Scottish patriot and general. In the early fourteenth century, he tried to drive the English out of Scotland. But he was unsuccessful because the English were too powerful. Finally, Bruce was forced to run away and to hide in a cave.

One day he lay on a cot in this cave, thinking of the sad state of Scotland. A spider began to weave a web above his head. Simply to amuse himself, Bruce reached up and broke the web. Immediately the spider began to weave a new one. Then six times in succession Bruce broke the web, and six times the spider immediately made a new one. Bruce marveled at such perseverance. He said to himself that he would break the web the seventh time. If the spider made a new one, it would be a good lesson to him, for, like the spider, he had been defeated six times in battle.

Bruce then broke the web, and again the spider made a new one.

From this simple incident, Bruce took heart. He again gathered an army, and this time he was successful in driving out the English.

Write the letter of the correct answer in the blank.

1. Robert Bruce was _____ .
   a. American   b. Scottish

2. He had to hide in a _____ .
   a. house   b. cave

3. The English were too _____ .
   a. powerful   b. weak

4. In the cave, he saw a _____ .
   a. spider   b. stone

5. Bruce broke the _____ .
   a. web   b. bottle

6. The spider _____ .
   a. quit   b. began again

7. Bruce had been defeated _____ times.
   a. seven   b. six

8. Bruce broke the web _____ times.
   a. seven   b. six

9. Bruce left the cave and gathered _____ .
   a. an army   b. some food

Answer Key

Exercise 1

A. 2. They're
    3. It's
    4. He's
    5. It's
    6. We're
    7. She's
    8. I'm
    9. You're
    10. They're

B. 2. is
    3. is
    4. are
    5. is
    6. are
    7. is
    8. are
    9. is
    10. is

Exercise 2

2. a. Is Ricardo angry with us?
   b. Ricardo isn't angry with us.
3. a. Are he and she good friends?
   b. He and she aren't good friends.
4. a. Is he very happy?
   b. He isn't very happy.
5. a. Are both sisters tall and athletic?
   b. Both sisters aren't tall and athletic.

6. a. Is she a clever girl?
   b. She isn't a clever girl.
7. a. Are they members of our club?
   b. They aren't members of our club.
8. a. Is he a good baseball player?
   b. He isn't a good baseball player.

Exercise 3

2. was
3. were
4. were
5. were
6. was

7. were
8. were
9. were
10. was
11. were

12. was, was
13. was
14. was
15. was
16. were

17. were
18. was
19. was
20. were
21. was

22. was
23. were
24. were
25. were

Exercise 4

2. a. Were the doors closed?
   b. The doors weren't closed.
3. a. Were the exercises difficult?
   b. The exercises weren't difficult.
4. a. Was the woman a stranger to her?
   b. The woman wasn't a stranger to her.
5. a. Was it a beautiful day?
   b. It wasn't a beautiful day.
6. a. Was the sea very calm?
   b. The sea wasn't very calm.
7. a. Was he a tall man?
   b. He wasn't a tall man.
8. a. Were there many difficult exercises in the lesson?
   b. There weren't many difficult exercises in the lesson.

Exercise 5

2. She'll be our new teacher.
3. Ms. Roth will be in New York.
4. They'll be good students.
5. This will be your desk.
6. There will be two soldiers in the room.
7. We'll be very tired after a long walk.
8. I'll be happy to be here.
9. You'll be angry with us.
10. The dog will be happy to see you.
11. Mr. Moreno will be out of town.
12. The wine will be very good this year.

Exercise 6

2. a. Will the test be easy?
   b. The test won't be easy.
3. a. Will they be here before noon?
   b. They won't be here before noon.
4. a. Will there be three tables in the room?
   b. There won't be three tables in the room.
5. a. Will he be happy to get home?
   b. He won't be happy to get home.
6. a. Will she be very angry?
   b. She won't be very angry.
7. a. Will Mr. Murphy be in class today?
   b. Mr. Murphy won't be in class today.
8. a. Will Nicholas be absent next week?
   b. Nicholas won't be absent next week.

Exercise 7

2. is stopping
3. is ringing
4. you're wearing
5. is crossing
6. is starting
7. is sleeping
8. is trying
9. is making
10. are beginning
11. is having
12. is playing
13. they're living
14. is managing
15. is watching
16. They're having
17. is watering
18. is spending

Exercise 8

2. a. Is it beginning to rain?
   b. It isn't beginning to rain.
3. a. Is the sky growing dark?
   b. The sky isn't growing dark.
4. a. Is he working for a new company?
   b. He isn't working for a new company.
5. a. Is Pete cleaning the room now?
   b. Pete isn't cleaning the room now.
6. a. Are the joggers turning the corner?
   b. The joggers aren't turning the corner.
7. a. Is she having lunch outside on the lawn?
   b. She isn't having lunch outside on the lawn.
8. a. Is Nora doing well in college?
   b. Nora isn't doing well in college.

Exercise 9

2. was raining
3. was having
4. were traveling
5. was sleeping
6. was ordering

7. were driving
8. was working
9. was taking
10. was talking
11. were staying

12. was getting
13. was going
14. was shining
15. was watching

Exercise 10

2. you'll be traveling
3. I'll be having
4. I'll be waiting
5. she'll be practicing
6. It'll be raining

7. I'll be working
8. we'll be flying
9. He'll be watching
10. She'll be taking
11. he'll be studying

12. they'll be having
13. they'll be watching
14. I'll be taking

Exercise 11

2. comes
3. walk
4. play
5. eat
6. works

7. like
8. chases
9. works
10. sits
11. play

12. prepares
13. eat
14. likes
15. take
16. travel

17. attends
18. speaks
19. go
20. waters
21. jogs

22. changes
23. takes

Exercice 12

A. 2. Ann does not like to study English.
3. They do not speak French well.
4. The plane does not leave at ten o'clock.
5. He does not know French perfectly.
6. I do not feel well today.

B. 2. I don't need air conditioning in my room.
3. We don't use many books every year.
4. I don't understand everything he says.
5. She doesn't want to visit Mexico.
6. He doesn't begin his new job on the fifteenth.

Exercise 13

2. Does he enjoy fishing?
3. Does she spend her vacation in the mountains?
4. Do they come to school by bus?
5. Does Andrew know how to play soccer?
6. Do the children wake up at about six o'clock every morning?
7. Does he know a lot about South America?
8. Do they go to the park every afternoon?
9. Do they have many friends in that school?
10. Do both boys swim well?
11. Do they live on the outskirts of the city?
12. Does Roy get up early every morning?

Exercise 14

2. listened	7. lasted	12. arrived	17. delivered	22. passed
3. talked	8. changed	13. watched	18. placed	23. turned off
4. wanted	9. liked	14. studied	19. walked	24. moved
5. lived	10. waited	15. mailed	20. cooked	
6. expected	11. painted	16. learned	21. waved	

Exercise 15

2. told	6. wrote	10. drank	14. knew	18. spoke, came
3. sat	7. saw	11. gave	15. felt	19. wrote, told
4. put	8. cost	12. sold	16. went	20. knew
5. began	9. had	13. heard	17. read	

Exercise 16

A. 2. They did not tell us the story.
   3. She did not put the books on his desk.
   4. We did not stay in Mexico City for two weeks.
   5. I did not see Florence yesterday.
   6. He did not plan his work well.

B. 2. I didn't know him very well.
   3. You didn't sell your new car.
   4. Mr. Wood didn't speak to Beth about the exam.
   5. She didn't come to the meeting alone.
   6. We didn't sit together at the concert last night.

Exercise 17

2. Did Don give her a VCR for Christmas?
3. Did we stay in Europe all year?
4. Did she tell us about her trip?
5. Did he enter this class in September?
6. Did they go by plane?
7. Did she come home very late?
8. Did they go to the party together?
9. Did they know each other as children?
10. Did Rose work there for many years?
11. Did Mr. Stein feel better after his operation?
12. Did the meeting begin on time?

Exercise 18

2. They'll see	7. I'll leave	12. We'll meet	17. will pay	22. will open
3. I'll give	8. will find	13. I'll pay	18. You'll spend	23. We'll be
4. She'll help	9. You'll need	14. You'll learn	19. I'll make	
5. will clean	10. will do	15. We'll remain	20. you'll find	
6. will close	11. will blow	16. he'll be	21. will give	

Exercise 19

A. 2. My boyfriend will not finish his degree next year.
  3. I will not be back tomorrow.
  4. The weather will not be cool tomorrow.
  5. Tom will not be able to meet us this evening.
  6. These exercises will not be difficult for you.

B. 2. She won't do well in that position.
  3. Gina won't teach all the grammar courses.
  4. Jim and I won't sign the contract tomorrow.
  5. They won't finish the work in April.
  6. The meeting won't last an hour.

Exercise 20

2. Will Ned come back at three o'clock?
3. Will the shop be open at six o'clock?
4. Will it cost six dollars to fix the lamp?
5. Will the plant die without sunshine?
6. Will they spend four months in Spain?
7. Will she meet us downtown?
8. Will they pay their bill next week?
9. Will the meeting begin at eight?
10. Will it last an hour?

Exercise 21

2. are going to have
3. am going to go
4. is going to leave
5. is going to visit
6. are going to speak
7. is going to study
8. is going to take
9. are going to wait
10. are going to fly
11. is going to study
12. are going to get
13. are going to go
14. is going to leave
15. are going to tear down
16. is going to go
17. are going to sell
18. is going to take
19. are going to buy
20. are going to do
21. is going to help
22. am going to wash

Exercise 22

2. a. Is Rose going to take a vacation?
  b. Rose is not going to take a vacation.
3. a. Are we going to go to the movies tonight?
  b. We're not going to go to the movies tonight.
4. a. Is he going to start working there on Monday?
  b. He's not going to start working there on Monday.
5. a. Are they going to pay him a good salary?
  b. They're not going to pay him a good salary.
6. a. Is Carmen going to move to California next month?
  b. Carmen is not going to move to California next month.
7. a. Is Henry going to travel to Europe on his vacation?
  b. Henry is not going to travel to Europe on his vacation.
8. a. Is she going to spend the weekend in Connecticut?
  b. She's not going to spend the weekend in Connecticut.

Exercise 23

2. have finished	7. have studied	12. has gone	16. has tried
3. has visited	8. have learned	13. has taught	17. has begun
4. has returned	9. has been	14. has seen	18. have grown
5. have lost	10. have heard	15. has made,	19. have been
6. have been	11. have lent	has lost	20. has visited

Exercise 24

2. a. Has she been there for many years?
   b. She hasn't been there for many years.
3. a. Have they waited there a long time?
   b. They haven't waited there a long time.
4. a. Has the movie been seen by millions of people?
   b. The movie hasn't been seen by millions of people.
5. a. Have Mr. and Mrs. Sato studied English?
   b. Mr. and Mrs. Sato haven't studied English.
6. a. Has Alan been absent?
   b. Alan hasn't been absent.
7. a. Have they found a pen?
   b. They haven't found a pen.
8. a. Has he been the best student all year?
   b. He hasn't been the best student all year.

Exercise 25

2. He has been selling cars for many years.
3. They have been traveling all over Europe.
4. She has been sleeping for more than ten hours.
5. It has been raining all day long.
6. He has been studying English for many years.
7. She has been catching fish in that stream for years.
8. He has been teaching English for ten years.
9. They have been living in Caracas since 1983.
10. The two nations have been quarreling for many years.

Exercise 26

2. had looked	7. had gone	12. had met	17. had visited
3. had worked	8. had worked	13. had had	18. had happened
4. had captured	9. had taken	14. had been	19. had expected
5. had prepared	10. had left	15. had misdirected	20. had decided
6. had found	11. had seen	16. had left	

Exercise 27

2. had been watching	7. had been working
3. had been living	8. had been going
4. had been drinking	9. had been running
5. had been swimming	10. had been playing
6. had been lying	11. had been walking

Exercise 28

2. will have died
3. will have finished
4. will have gone
5. will have left
6. will have finished
7. will have been
8. will have forgotten
9. will have learned
10. will have forgotten
11. will have seen
12. will have arrived
13. will have finished
14. will have lost
15. will have done
16. will have completed
17. will have eaten
18. will have changed
19. will have become

Exercise 29

2. is teaching
3. was working
4. will have
5. came
6. was coming, met, asked
7. have been
8. is playing
9. had seen
10. have read
11. will have completed
12. came, was leaving
13. was shining
14. begins
15. go
16. is knocking
17. has been heard
18. has studied
19. studied
20. will come
21. was studying
22. were driving, had
23. jumped
24. had called, had left
25. fell, was crossing

Exercise 30

2. We didn't go to the movies last night.
3. You ought not to tell him.
4. He shouldn't go there sooner.
5. I haven't lived there for many years.
6. They weren't supposed to leave yesterday.
7. She can't speak French perfectly.
8. The mechanic won't be back by eight o'clock.
9. He didn't have to work late last night.
10. My friend doesn't live in Los Angeles.
11. She isn't the best student in our class.
12. You may not smoke here.
13. There weren't many students absent from class yesterday.
14. They weren't driving very fast at the time.

Exercise 31

2. Can Mr. Ralston speak Chinese fluently?
3. Should she spend more time at home?
4. May he sit in this chair?
5. Can they meet us in Los Angeles?
6. Can't her brother-in-law drive?
7. Should Ruth eat less candy?
8. Must you tell her the truth?
9. Should we speak to her about it?
10. May they leave now?
11. Can the entire tour group go by van?
12. Must you send them a telegram?
13. Should she work at home?
14. May she wait in the office?

Exercise 32

2. How many months are there in a year?
3. Where may she wait?
4. What time did the jet arrive?
5. What time is it now?
6. How did he go to Chicago?
7. What time must she leave?
8. Where are they right now?
9. How much did the book cost?
10. Where do they work now?
11. How long did her supervisor live in Tokyo?
12. What time did he get up this morning?
13. How long did they sit in the park?
14. How well does she understand English?

Exercise 33

2. They're	7. We're	12. It's	17. I'm
3. I'll	8. They're	13. There's	18. There's
4. I've	9. It's	14. She's	19. They'll
5. We'll	10. It's	15. He's	20. It's
6. She'll	11. They've	16. You're	21. You'll

Exercise 34

2. a. Yes, she does.   b. No, she doesn't.
3. a. Yes, I have.   b. No, I haven't.
4. a. Yes, it is.   b. No, it isn't.
5. a. Yes, they will.   b. No, they won't.
6. a. Yes, they are.   b. No, they aren't.
7. a. Yes, she did.   b. No, she didn't.
8. a. Yes, it was.   b. No, it wasn't.
9. a. Yes, it is.   b. No, it isn't.
10. a. Yes, we should.   b. No, we shouldn't.
11. a. Yes, you may.   b. No, you may not.
12. a. Yes, he can.   b. No, he can't.
13. a. Yes, it did.   b. No, it didn't.

Exercise 35

2. doesn't she	7. won't there	12. did you	17. are they
3. was it	8. didn't she	13. can she	18. is it
4. has it	9. hasn't it	14. don't they	19. could he
5. isn't it	10. will you	15. aren't you	20. didn't I
6. are you	11. doesn't he	16. don't you	21. has it

Exercise 36

A.
2. to be enjoying
3. to be doing
4. to be spending
5. to be doing
6. to be learning
7. to be working
8. to be having
9. to be doing

B.
2. to have met
3. to have made
4. to have arrived
5. to have enjoyed
6. to have understood
7. to have missed
8. to have missed
9. to have been

Exercise 37

2. wait
3. to take
4. look/to look
5. come
6. to leave
7. leave
8. fall
9. wait
10. touch
11. take
12. to know
13. play
14. write/to write
15. laugh
16. to be
17. play
18. see

Exercise 38

2. The heavy box was carried by him.
3. The president was recognized immediately.
4. My umbrella has been stolen.
5. The merchandise will be delivered in the morning.
6. The portrait had already been finished.
7. The work was finished in time.
8. The cries of wolves were heard in the distance.
9. A young tiger was found in the open field.
10. The tiger was frightened by the shot.
11. Some water will be brought from the well.

Exercise 39

2. We were taught two languages.
3. We were asked to come early.
4. The man was given a reward of a hundred dollars.
5. She will be sent flowers.
6. We were shown the principal spots of interest.
7. I was told the news.
8. Everyone has been asked the same question.
9. The police were informed of his whereabouts.
10. Each of us has been promised a raise.
11. We will surely be asked about the accident.

Exercise 40

2. He was being sent to school.
3. The case is being argued now.
4. A new subway is being built in that city.
5. Some chairs are being put in that room, aren't they?
6. A letter is being written now, isn't it?
7. The building across the street is being torn down.
8. The plants are being watered.
9. The verdict is being discussed now.
10. Many new buildings were being constructed in Caracas when I was there.
11. Both contracts are being drawn up today.
12. The streets are being kept much cleaner now.

Exercise 41

2. The box should be sent to Philadelphia.
3. The engine has to be started first.
4. A new group may be organized.
5. My appointment ought to be canceled.
6. The meeting cannot be held in that room.
7. The mattress may be delivered while you're out.
8. The bill has to be paid by the first of the month.
9. The other bills must be paid by the end of the month.
10. The plants ought to be watered once a week.

Exercise 42

2. My history teacher was not born in Philadelphia.
3. The garden was not watered.
4. The mail is not delivered at ten o'clock.
5. His car was not stolen from in front of his house.
6. The goods will not be delivered on Wednesday.
7. The thief was not sent to prison.
8. The president is not elected every four years.
9. The children were not put to bed.
10. The battle will not be fought tomorrow.
11. The table has not been moved.
12. She was not given the best grade.

Exercise 43

2. Is she interested in Spanish?
3. Will they be worn out after such a long trip?
4. Is Donna interested in teaching aerobics?
5. Are they concerned about his lack of strength?
6. Will Dave be anxious to hear the rest of the story?
7. Are the stores always closed at this hour?
8. Has the electricity been turned off?
9. Were both doors closed?
10. Was he very much discouraged by his failures?
11. Was Roberta very upset by the news?
12. Were they surprised by his behavior?
13. Is her arm broken in three places?

Exercise 44

2. may	6. would	10. were crossing	14. was	18. wanted
3. can	7. meant	11. was going	15. doesn't	19. might
4. could	8. has	12. would	16. kept	20. had
5. could	9. will	13. is	17. had died	21. remembered

Exercise 45

2. Tomiko said that she knew his name.
3. Nick said that it was getting late.
4. He said that we would have to hurry.
5. Watson said that it looked like rain.
6. Monique said that she had read that book.
7. Sue said that she could call them by telephone.
8. Bijan said that he had to go to the customs office.
9. The man said that he needed some money for soup and coffee.

Exercise 46

2. Ms. Cruz asked if I liked New York.
3. She asked what time it was.
4. Melanie asked where Busch Gardens was.
5. He asked if Paolo sang well.
6. The man asked how I was.
7. My professor asked where Room 16 was.
8. She asked why I smoked.
9. The teacher asked where Andorra was.
10. She asked if it was going to rain.

Exercise 47

2. They told me not to go.
3. I told him to leave me alone.
4. You told him to close the door.
5. She told me not to turn off the radio.
6. Anne told David to sit down.
7. He told her to think it over.
8. They told me to come back later.
9. My father told us not to jump on the bed.
10. He told her not to come late.
11. My doctor told him to take two aspirin and plenty of vitamin C.
12. She told him not to tell the answer.

Exercise 48

2. He has his shoes shined.
3. Sarah had her sweater pressed.
4. Larry had his old van overhauled.
5. I must have my watch fixed.
6. The front office had those letters mailed.
7. We must have our apartment painted.
8. The tenant must have the apartment painted.
9. Ms. Jackson wants to have her typewriter cleaned.
10. She is going to have her nails manicured.
11. You want to have your shoes resoled.
12. I have had the water tank filled.
13. My mother had her rose garden weeded.

Exercise 49

2. How handsome he is!
3. What a bright young lady her oldest daughter is!
4. How quickly they have learned English!
5. What a beautiful new car you have!
6. How well Helen drives!
7. How tall Ryan has grown!
8. What a charming city Paris is!
9. What good taste she has!
10. What a gorgeous home they have!
11. What a lucky fellow he is!

Exercise 50

2. She thought he did know the song.
3. Fred didn't come, but he did telephone.
4. I did like it very much.
5. Do come back later.
6. Do visit us again sometime.
7. She does enjoy her lessons.
8. We did do these exercises.
9. I don't like movies, but I do like the theater.
10. Do tell us all about it.
11. He did try to please us.
12. We don 't make much money, but we do have a lot of fun.
13. I do know a lot of Japanese phrases.

Exercise 51

2. I don't think so.
3. I believe so.
4. I don't think so.
5. I believe so.

6. I'm afraid so.
7. I believe so.
8. I hope so.
9. I hope so.

10. I think so.
11. I believe so.
12. I don't believe so.

Exercise 52

2. there is!
3. they have!
4. he must!
5. he has!
6. she is!

7. it is!
8. she is!
9. she does!
10. there are!
11. it is!

12. it can!
13. he can't!
14. they will!
15. it is!
16. they are!

17. you are!
18. it is!
19. she has!

Exercise 53

2. does
3. did
4. are
5. will

6. did
7. has
8. did
9. is

10. will
11. did
12. is
13. have

14. did
15. are
16. is
17. do

18. were
19. is
20. will
21. does

Exercise 54

A. 2. He didn't go, and I didn't, either.
   3. He didn't study, and Marc didn't, either.
   4. She won't be there, and her sister won't, either.
   5. Dolores hasn't heard the tape, and you haven't, either.
   6. You can't speak Latin, and Desmond can't, either.

B. 1. Jane wasn't at the lesson, and neither was her friend.
   2. Marta doesn't know them, and neither do we.
   3. Your watch doesn't have the right time, and neither does my watch/mine.
   4. She hasn't seen him, and neither have I.
   5. Paula never rests, and neither does Mindy.
   6. He wouldn't say that, and neither would I.

Exercise 55

2. is supposed to come
3. were supposed to deliver
4. was supposed to send
5. was supposed to send
6. am supposed to write
7. is supposed to be
8. is supposed to take
9. is supposed to be
10. was supposed to telephone
11. is supposed to be
12. are supposed to read
13. is supposed to call
14. am supposed to arrive
15. is supposed to meet
16. is supposed to spend
17. is supposed to know
18. was supposed to publish
19. am supposed to get up
20. are supposed to put
21. is supposed to prepare
22. are supposed to go
23. is supposed to be

Exercise 56

2. He used to work here.
3. She used to come to class on time.
4. Monica used to be an industrious student.
5. He used to ride the subway to work.
6. Colette used to bring me flowers every day.
7. Mike used to play the trumpet very well.
8. He used to study hard.
9. My advisor used to help me very much.
10. I used to live on Forty-sixth Street.
11. Her father used to go to that college.
12. I used to know her well.

Exercise 57

3. used to
4. are used to
5. used to
6. is used to
7. am used to
8. used to
9. used to
10. is used to
11. are used to
12. used to
13. used to
14. is used to
15. used to
16. am used to
17. used to
18. are used to
19. used to
20. is used to
21. is used to
22. used to
23. used to
24. is used to

Exercise 58

2. He'd better see a doctor.
3. Sue had better rest for a while.
4. You'd better take private lessons.
5. They'd better save a little money for a change.
6. Peter had better not mention this to anyone.
7. You'd better give up smoking.
8. She'd better stop seeing him.
9. Dennis had better memorize these facts.
10. Your lawyer had better call my lawyer.
11. However, we'd better not give them too many details.

Exercise 59

2. She'd rather come back later.
3. He'd rather watch TV.
4. They'd rather walk to school.
5. Dan would rather do all his homework before he leaves school.
6. I'd rather stay home tonight and watch television.
7. Betty would rather drive a big car.
8. We'd rather spend the summer at home instead of in the country.
9. He'd rather not speak to her about the matter again.
10. Marie would rather not mention it to anyone.
11. She'd rather study in this class instead of the advanced class.

Exercise 60

2. They thought they could raise the money.
3. She thought she could speak English as well as I.
4. He hoped he could get back here by five o'clock.
5. They felt that they could talk to you in confidence.
6. She insisted she could convince him.
7. We thought we could finish this book by June.
8. She said she could marry a doctor.
9. I couldn't get back before noon.
10. He couldn't leave this book here.

Exercise 61

2. If you should pass a mailbox, please mail this letter.
3. If that letter should arrive, bring it to my office at once.
4. If Dad should hear about it, I won't be able to go.
5. If you should hear the rumor, don't believe it.
6. If the electricity should go off, we will have to work in the dark.
7. If the weather should turn cold, we will be in an awful fix.
8. If the dog should bite her, she'll probably sue us.
9. If a police officer should see you driving that way, you'll get a ticket.
10. If you should break the glass, you'll have to buy another.
11. If you should be free tomorrow, we'll go to a movie.

Exercise 62

A.
2. rises
3. raises
4. raised
5. rose
6. risen
7. raise
8. rose
9. raised
10. raise

B.
2. sat
3. set
4. sit
5. set
6. set
7. sitting
8. sit

Exercise 63

A.
2. lay
3. lay
4. lain
5. laid
6. lying
7. laid
8. Lie
9. laid
10. lying

B.
2. rose
3. rises
4. set
5. laid
6. lie
7. raise
8. rising
9. raise
10. lying

Exercise 64

2. Having finished the work, she left.
3. Seeing her, I cried with joy.
4. Having spoken to her, he was very happy.
5. Having been seen by her, he had to admit everything.
6. Leaving the party, we ran into Joyce and Tom.
7. Having left here, they went to another party.
8. The soldiers, being forced to march, pretended to be ill.
9. The men, having been taken captive, finally escaped.
10. The day, having been a sad one, finally ended.

Exercise 65

2. driving
3. going
4. waiting
5. buying
6. traveling
7. coming
8. holding
9. receiving
10. painting
11. hitting
12. taking
13. going
14. making
15. breaking
16. turning
17. going
18. working
19. planting
20. cleaning

Exercise 66

2. of waiting
3. in hearing
4. for trying
5. of losing
6. of leaving
7. in finding
8. in meeting
9. in speaking
10. of swimming
11. on driving
12. to meeting
13. of working
14. of losing
15. of finishing
16. of mentioning
17. of seeing
18. in doing
19. from continuing
20. of finding
21. for doing
22. in helping

Exercise 67

A.
1. despite
2. despite
3. despite
4. despite
5. Despite

B.
1. in spite of
2. In spite of
3. in spite of
4. In spite of
5. in spite of

C. 1.–9. Individual answers

Exercise 68

2. The last lesson was difficult, but this one is easy.
3. This chair is very comfortable, but that one is not.
4. They have two black cats and three white ones.
5. You were asking about a black notebook. Is this the one that you lost?
6. I like all games, but tennis and basketball are the ones I like best.
7. We find that it is more fun to take several short trips than one long one.
8. There were boats of all sizes in the bay, big ones and little ones.
9. We took pictures of almost everything, but the ones we took of the bullfight turned out best.
10. This record is scratched; please give me a new one.

Exercise 69

2. thirsty
3. foolish
4. quarrelsome
5. manly
6. childish
7. greedy
8. wiry
9. talented
10. hourly
11. sunny
12. cloudy
13. revolutionary
14. hungry
15. daily
16. peaceful
17. needy
18. dirty
19. cultured
20. beautiful
21. dead
22. flowery
23. weekly
24. monthly
25. tasty
26. summery
27. wintry
28. Danish
29. Irish
30. Scottish
31. Swedish
32. Swiss
33. Turkish
34. Spanish
35. Mexican
36. American
37. Canadian
38. Indian
39. Greek
40. Polish

Exercise 70

2. anger
3. depth
4. happiness
5. height
6. convenience
7. ugliness
8. possibility
9. width
10. sarcasm
11. absence
12. danger
13. weakness
14. strength
15. emphasis
16. silence
17. intelligence
18. generosity
19. jealousy
20. anxiety
21. desperation
22. greatness
23. beauty
24. roughness
25. death
26. loudness
27. selfishness
28. cynic/cynicism
29. presence
30. deceit
31. bitterness
32. sweetness
33. electricity
34. dryness
35. heat
36. bashfulness
37. pride
38. dreariness
39. truth
40. clarity

Exercise 71

2. as far as	9. as far as	16. as far as
3. as far as	10. until	17. until
4. until	11. as far as	18. as far as
5. as far as	12. as far as	19. until
6. until	13. as far as	20. until
7. As far as	14. until	
8. until	15. until	

Exercise 72

2. I saw him on the street yesterday.
3. She usually comes to the lesson on time.
4. Luisa prepared her lesson well last night.
5. I often see him on the street.
6. My uncle generally reads *Time* magazine every week.
7. We usually go for a walk in the park on Sunday.
8. My friends and I went for a stroll in the park last Sunday.
9. She never takes an early train.
10. I seldom drink milk.

Exercise 73

2. anymore	11. still
3. anymore	12. anymore
4. still	13. still
5. anymore	14. still, anymore
6. still	15. still, still
7. anymore	16. anymore
8. anymore	17. still
9. still, anymore	18. still, anymore
10. still	19. anymore, still

Exercise 74

2. Nobody else helped him with the work.
3. You must ask somebody else about it.
4. Who else knows the combination?
5. They have never sold that merchandise anywhere else.
6. Did you see anything else that you liked?
7. Let's do something else tonight besides watch television.
8. I didn't tell anybody else about it.
9. How else can I paint the room?

Exercise 75

2. Whoever
3. whenever
4. whatever
5. whatever
6. whenever
7. whatever
8. Whoever
9. wherever
10. Whenever
11. wherever/whenever
12. whenever
13. wherever
14. whichever, when-ever
15. whenever
16. whenever
17. Whenever
18. Whoever
19. Whatever

Exercise 76

2. many
3. much
4. a lot of
5. few
6. little
7. little
8. few
9. much
10. few
11. little
12. a lot of
13. many
14. much
15. many
16. a lot of
17. many
18. much
19. many
20. much

Exercise 77

2. Nick's
3. are
4. me
5. them
6. comes Phil
7. me
8. themselves
9. a
10. an
11. an
12. them away
13. her up
14. she comes
15. them
16. a
17. a
18. an
19. her
20. me
21. herself
22. ourselves
23. yours
24. my

Exercise 78

2. about/of
3. in
4. to/with
5. for
6. to
7. for
8. in
9. from
10. by
11. to
12. to
13. at
14. to
15. in
16. from
17. at
18. at/for
19. from
20. from

Exercise 79

2. The woman you were speaking to is my teacher.
3. That is the store I lost my purse in.
4. She is the kind of representative it is difficult to get away from.
5. The adviser you should speak to is Dr. Kojima.
6. It is a subject we will never agree on.
7. The thing they were arguing about was really of little importance.
8. It is a place you will feel at home in.
9. It was Charles I had to wait so long for.
10. It was Jack he borrowed the money from.
11. The room we study in is on the second floor.
12. This is the street they live on.

Exercise 80

2. effect
3. effects
4. advise
5. into
6. stole
7. somewhat
8. affected
9. advice
10. somewhat
11. stole
12. robbed
13. in

Exercise 81

2. taught
3. have I
4. beside
5. teach
6. beside
7. taught
8. pet
9. did he mention
10. wait
11. could you
12. to go
13. seen

Exercise 82

2. no
3. won
4. not
5. spilled
6. poured
7. Not
8. poured
9. won
10. pour
11. No
12. Not

Exercise 83

2. The, the, the
3. a, a, a, The, a, ____
4. ____ , ____
5. the, ____ , the
6. a, the
7. The, ____ , the, ____
8. the, the, ____
9. ____ , The
10. ____ , the, the
11. the, ____ , the, ____
12. ____ , the, the
13. the, the
14. ____ , the
15. ____ , ____ , ____ , ____ , ____
16. the, ____
17. The, ____ , ____
18. The

Exercise 84

1. We study history, mathematics, geography, and reading.
2. Sue Bielski, the mechanic, repaired our car and also fixed our refrigerator.
3. He was, of course, more to be pitied than censured.
4. Mike Madison, the head of the company, will see you on Sunday.
5. The governor, in the first place, did not pardon the murderer.
6. He was born in Scranton, Pennsylvania, on March 23, 1980, and he has lived there ever since.
7. We cannot, after all, live forever.
8. By the way, do you remember Mrs. Jackson's telephone number?
9. Sue Brown, Henry's cousin, is visiting him at the latter's camp in Stroudsburg, Pennsylvania.
10. Where were you, Miss Lyons, on the morning of June 26, 1983?
11. The old Amos Building, a famous landmark of the town, was recently torn down. As a matter of fact, it was town down on February 12, Lincoln's Birthday.
12. The most popular summer sports are tennis, swimming, and hiking.
13. Yesterday, I met three former schoolmates, Tom Beck, Ruth Sanchez, and Randy Owens.
14. The last time I saw them was on August 3, 1982.

Exercise 85

1. If it rains, we may have to postpone our trip.
2. I may, if the weather is bad, cancel the class trip.
3. We may have to postpone our trip if it rains.
4. When he protested so vigorously, we withdrew our proposal.
5. Because he was so widely read, he had a comprehensive grasp of the entire subject.
6. Our work being over for the day, we closed shop and went home.
7. Because he had been ill, he asked to be excused from all assignments.
8. If Monica wanted, she could be a very good student.
9. Yoshiko, having gotten a visa, bought the airline ticket.
10. He never studied any foreign language when he was in high school.
11. When he was in high school, he never studied any foreign language.
12. He never, when he was in high school, studied any foreign language.
13. Although she was a skilled engineer, she did not know the first thing about road building.
14. Natasha was, as was easily seen from her speech, a woman of strong opinions.

Exercise 86

1. Barbara, who is quite smart, deserves to pass.
2. Any student who is lazy does not deserve to pass.
3. Any girl who has brown hair will be all right for the part of the heroine.
4. Angela, who has brown hair, was selected for the part of the heroine.
5. Daniel's hands, feet, and face, which were covered with mud, were washed by Mother.
6. Any passenger who enters the engine room does so at his or her own risk.
7. The person who said that is mistaken.
8. Eva, who told the story, was obviously misinformed.
9. Wednesday, when my brother is usually out of town, will be a good day to call.
10. Ms. Rubio, who was in the real estate business, decided to promote Glen Acres, which was formerly a swamp.
11. The fellow who was laughing was clearly the perpetrator of the joke.
12. His great love for nature, which he acquired during his childhood, showed itself in his curiosity about any bird which flew through his garden.
13. The profit which you can expect on so cheap an article is very small.
14. We heard a noise that resembled the cry of an injured animal.
15. The George Washington Bridge, which spans the Hudson River, has been very successful financially.
16. Kyle, unlike his brother Josh, has brown hair, blue eyes, and a light complexion.

Exercise 87

1. Chicago is my favorite city, but Philadelphia offers more advantages.
2. Fools need advice; only wise men profit by it.
3. The general manager will talk to you soon and will give you the information.
4. Alec is a very good automobile mechanic, and his prices are low.
5. I had the passport for a week, but then finally I returned it.
6. She kept the book for a long time, but she finally returned it.
7. Bill had the ring; then he gave it to Joe.
8. There were six ambassadors, and their entrance was truly magnificent.
9. Marcia didn't go, but Colleen did.
10. Mary was highly pleased with the results; therefore, she showed her pleasure and gave us all a quarter.
11. Lou was pleased with the results, but Mr. Martin obviously wasn't.
12. Cowards die many times, but a brave man dies but once.
13. Marianne was cautious, but Henry bet on the black horse and won more than twenty dollars.
14. Tom plays the bass, and Dennis plays the acoustic guitar.
15. I like Trivial Pursuit; my sister likes Monopoly.
16. He was tattered and dirty, but he ate like a gentleman.
17. My brother or my mother will help you and will gladly show you the way.

Exercise 88

1. The changes which we are planning will soon be completed.
2. Jenny and Alice came into the room, looked around, whispered to each other, and then walked out.
3. William's store, which sells many fancy groceries, was recently repainted, and as a consequence, it now looks very nice.
4. "I am sure, Sophie," said Henry, "you will like our new summer place, which was built by the local company."
5. "Of course, Father, it's a pity," said Ellen, "that people don't appreciate the excellent work that you have done here."
6. We drove from Harrisburg, Pa., to Albany, which is the captial of New York State.
7. Mary and Ellen stopped and watched Henry and Joseph running and jumping.
8. We, Mary, Ethel, and I, considered going, but later we changed our minds and decided to stay home and rest.
9. The woman whom we saw yesterday was Don Gray's sister, Terry Nelson, who is a psychologist.
10. Saturday, Jan. 16 was the coldest day that we had, but the next day seemed even colder to me.
11. Everyone got into the van, we started out, and soon we were on the freeway.
12. At eleven, Rex adjourned the meeting, no decision having been reached by that time.
13. "I believe," said the visitor, "that Mr. Davis should be notified at once, yet we all realize that the duty is not a pleasant one."
14. Strangely enough, Heather and Jennifer came into the room, looked at the table, sat down, and began to read.
15. She is very intelligent, but the lack of a diploma would prevent her from entering any college, even one of low standards.

Exercise 90

1. a	3. b	5. a	7. a
2. b	4. b	6. b	8. b

Exercise 91

1. b	3. a	5. b	7. a
2. a	4. b	6. b	

Exercise 92

1. b	5. a	9. b
2. a	6. b	10. a
3. b	7. a	
4. b	8. b	

Exercise 93

1. a
2. a
3. b
4. b

5. a
6. a
7. b

Exercise 94

1. a
2. a
3. b
4. b

5. b
6. a

Exercise 95

1. a
2. b
3. b
4. b

5. a
6. a
7. b

Exercise 96

1. b
2. b
3. a

4. a
5. a
6. b

7. b
8. a
9. a